C000091726

Sussex
MURDERS

W.H. Johnson

SUTTON PUBLISHING

First published in the United Kingdom in 2005 by
Sutton Publishing Limited · Phoenix Mill
Thrupp · Stroud · Gloucestershire · GL5 2BU

Copyright © W.H. Johnson, 2005

Series Consulting Editor: Stewart P. Evans

All rights reserved. No part of this publication may be reproduced, stored in a
retrieval system, or transmitted, in any form or by any means, electronic,
mechanical, photocopying, recording or otherwise, without the prior permission of
the publisher and copyright holders.

W.H. Johnson has asserted the moral right to be identified as the author of this
work.

British Library Cataloguing in Publication Data
A catalogue record for this book is available from the British Library.

ISBN 0-7509-4127-8

Typeset in 10.5/13.5 Sabon.
Typesetting and origination by
Sutton Publishing Limited.
Printed and bound in England by
J.H. Haynes & Co. Ltd, Sparkford.

CONTENTS

ACKNOWLEDGEMENTS

My grateful thanks go to: Alan Skinner of Eastbourne for his photography and his driving; John Dibley for his energetic pursuit of details of the police career of Francis Fagan; John Kay for his 1986 article in *Ringmer History* 4, which was the basis of the chapter on the Ringmer case; Paul Williams for his Murder Files service which, as ever, has saved me much research time; Jonathan Goodman for his compelling talk on the Brighton Trunk Murders at the Police History Society's 1993 conference; Simon and Stephanie at The Wheel at Burwash Weald for the nineteenth-century photograph of the pub; Gordon Franks for sending the material relating to Henry Solomon; Andy Gammon for so willingly and speedily providing a photograph of the Law Courts at Lewes; Vivien Burgess for her help with the illustrations; the staffs of the East Sussex Record Office and the West Sussex Record Office; the staff of East Sussex Libraries service and particularly those at Lewes and Eastbourne; the staff of the Brighton History Centre; and all those who initiated the Brighton Police Museum.

None of the above is in any way responsible for any flaws, misinterpretations or inaccuracies in the following pages.

INTRODUCTION

Each of the murder cases dealt with in this book occurred in Sussex but they could have taken place anywhere at any time. Only one achieved national notoriety; others had no more than a fleeting local fame. Several of them have not previously appeared in book form, although, if only for a brief season, they filled column inches in the press and have since been forgotten. But they deserve to be better known.

All of these cases have their highly charged, dramatic moments, which is one of the fascinations of murder. In these pages, John Holloway goes about his awful work in the cottage at Donkey Row; in Gladish Wood, two men, one a grieving father, carry a corpse at dead of night; and at Sherry's, Toni Mancini dances the hours away, keeping the secret of his lover's fate to himself. And there are poignant moments, too, as when we catch only the most fleeting glimpse of Mrs Probert, listening to the judge pass the dread sentence on her husband or when we sense betrayal of trust as at Gun Hill, where poor William French goes home looking forward to his supper just as, years earlier, James Whale at Broadbridge Heath had trusted his young wife and her hasty pudding.

For most of us, distanced from such events, there is some challenge in trying to analyse the motives of those who murder and the risks they take in the commission of their crimes. The deaths of Galley and Chater, both old men, serve as an example of eighteenth-century organised crime protecting its empire, but this vile crime is also a more universal illustration of how some men enjoy cruelty for its own sake. Even so, in some of the cases, any satisfactory conclusion is difficult to arrive at: could we ever come to an understanding of the events leading up to the deaths of five people in a house at Eastbourne? What can have lain behind the actions of the man known as Robert Hicks Murray?

There are other mysteries, too, unsolved cases, some with outcomes that after so many years still leave doubts. How Joan Woodhouse met her end in Arundel Park is still a subject of debate; at Ringmer pond there remains the question: did she slip or was she pushed? And what about the weakly youth, Fred Parker? Ought he to have hanged? How much blame attached to him for the brutal killing of an old man?

What is it that leads us to want to know more about these people, some of them, though not all, wicked and cruel beyond belief? Can it be that in studying them, their motives, their situations, we learn something more about ourselves and our own lives? Is it that through them we can sometimes address our own darkest thoughts, peering over a precipice into a pit where we vaguely discern some meaning from their disturbing deeds?

Perhaps it is simpler than that. Whatever murder is, there is no escaping the fact that it frequently offers a compelling narrative. I hope that the chapters that follow will demonstrate this.

THE GENUINE
HISTORY

Of the Inhuman and Unparalell'd

𝔐𝔲𝔯𝔡𝔢𝔯𝔰

Committed on the BODIES of

Mr. *WILLIAM GALLEY*,

A Custom-House Officer in the Port of *Southampton*: And

Mr. *DANIEL CHATER*,

A Shoemaker, of *Fordingbridge* in *Hampshire*.

TOGETHER WITH

An Account of the Trials of the 𝔖𝔢𝔳𝔢𝔫 𝔅𝔩𝔬𝔬𝔡𝔶 𝔠𝔯𝔦𝔪𝔦𝔫𝔞𝔩𝔰, at CHICHESTER, by Virtue of a Special Commission, on the 16th, 17th and 18th of *January* 1748 : By which it appears, there never was such a Horrible Scene of Villainy ever heard of or known in the World before.

With a Particular Account of their Behaviour while under Confinement at *Chichester*, both before, at, and after Sentence of Death was pass'd upon them : Together with their Dying Words and Behaviour at the Place of Execution, which was at 3 o'Clock, on *Thursday*, *Jan.* 19. 1748-9.

Written by a GENTLEMAN at *Chichester* ;

And Publish'd at the Request of the Gentlemen of the County of *Sussex*, in Order to prevent the World from being amus'd with false and fictitious Relations.

LONDON:

Printed for the Proprietor, and published by B. DICKINSON, at the Corner of the *Bell-Savage Inn*, *Ludgate-Hill*. 1749. [Price Six Pence.]

This Pamphlet is entered in the Hall-Book of the Company of Stationers, and at the Stamp-Office ; and whoever shall presume to pyrate it, or any Part thereof, will be prosecuted as the Law directs.

The front cover of a 1749 pamphlet which recounted the sorry tale of William Galley and Daniel Chater.

1

THE MURDERS OF CHATER & GALLEY

Harting Coombe & Lady Holt Park, 1748

There is a myth that tells of a Merrie England, of some Golden Age when the English countryman, that Noble Savage, dwelt in peace and harmony with his neighbour. Perhaps in the great cities, the Londons, the Bristols, there was vice, corruption, brutality, but, so the story goes, in the pastures and sheepfolds, in the villages and market towns, the idyll was undisturbed.

Not so. Not in any century. And not in Sussex nor in its adjoining counties. Yet the romantic gloss of the old tales remains. We hear of gallant highwaymen, though these were few. We learn of daring pirates (naturally our own and not the dastardly French) and, most romantic of all, daring smugglers. But none of these bears much scrutiny and all that is required to dispel the legend of smuggling is to recount the last days of Daniel Chater and William Galley, victims in 1748 of what must rank among the vilest murders in the calendar of crime.

For centuries a brisk smuggling trade operated between France and the south coast of England. It developed into a highly professional, greatly sophisticated commercial venture, employing thousands of people – an estimated 20,000 in Sussex – at different levels, from the young farm lads who loaded and lifted the incoming and outgoing goods to those who led teams of pack horses by hidden ways from one safe house to another, from barns to midnight churchyards. There were the armed escorts, men with cutlasses and horse-pistols and heavy batons, all fit and ready to take on the military or the riding-officers who might dare to hinder their progress. And truth to tell, not all wished the trade to end, for how else could they have cheap tea, spirits and tobacco?

Such operations, carried on all over the southern counties, could never have succeeded without an intelligence web to support them, and such systems cannot operate without money to corrupt the forces of law. Out of this huge industry massive fortunes were made. Small wonder, then, that the great corrupt framework on which smuggling depended was held in place by the most ruthless treatment of any who might seek to bring it down. This great criminal conspiracy was sustained by a merciless violence. The murders of Chater and Galley were supreme examples of the smugglers at their worst. But it was these murders that were to break the Hawkhurst Gang, the leading group among the loose confederation of smugglers across Kent, Sussex and Hampshire.

It was this murder that seemed to coincide with the belated determination on the part of the authorities to bring the smugglers to book for they had become far too powerful. Parliament had commissioned a report in 1745 into 'the most infamous practice of smuggling', for it appeared that the smugglers were now a law unto themselves. 'The smuglers [*sic*] will, one time or another, if not prevented, be the ruin of this kingdom.' At last it was recognised that the general peace of the country was endangered by bands of men who ignored the law and those who endeavoured to implement it.

In August 1747, only months before the murders, a correspondent in Horsham writes, 'the outlawed and other smugglers in this and the neighbouring Counties are so numerous and desperate that the inhabitants are in continual fear of the mischiefs which these horrid wretches not only threaten but actually perpetrate all round the Country side'. Even so, some of the smugglers were regarded as local heroes by many; they were cult figures; they were famous, bold; they defied authority.

For example, they carried out an audacious plan in the autumn of 1747. On 4 October, men from the Hawkhurst gang, led by Thomas Kingsmill, met in Charlton Forest near Goodwood to concoct a scheme with a group of Dorset and Hampshire smugglers. Two days later, at eleven o'clock at night, after a second meeting at Rowland's Castle, thirty smugglers mounted guard in the area leading to the Customs House at Poole while another thirty, armed with axes and crowbars, broke in. Imagine the nerve of it! They smashed the locks, wrenched off the bolts, hammered down the

Smugglers break open the Customs House, Poole, 1747.

doors and made off with thirty hundredweight of tea valued then at £500. It was rightfully theirs, they claimed. The tea and thirty-nine casks of brandy and rum which they had, weeks earlier, bought in Guernsey had been seized at sea by a revenue ship on its way to the Dorset coast and lodged in the Customs House. But wasn't it really their property? And how dare the customs service take it from them! Their mission accomplished, the men rode off triumphantly, each carrying five 27lb bags of tea.

Later in the morning, many villagers along the way turned out to greet the gang of mounted rascals as they passed, to wave and cheer them as they rode unhindered along the road. And it was at Fordingbridge, where they paused for breakfast and adulation, that Jack Diamond looked into the crowd and spotted the shoemaker, Daniel Chater, a man he had worked with on the harvest some time past. Diamond shook the old man by the hand and gave him a small bag of tea. It was the first step towards Chater's murder.

By the time the local authorities had roused themselves there was no sign of the smugglers but their coup echoed throughout the south. The Government might make noises about the smuggling trade, about its pernicious effects, but it seemed as deep-rooted as ever, quite beyond control. And local people were tight-lipped, many of them grudging towards the authorities, others mindful that if they told what they knew they would suffer, for the smuggling gangs showed little mercy to those who passed on information about them. Nevertheless, the authorities went about their business in the hope that something might emerge. And it did. Daniel Chater did not keep quiet about the bag of tea he had been given by Jack Diamond. Perhaps he bragged that he knew one of the great men, said that he was an acquaintance of one of those who had been to Poole. Even the dissolute great attract admiration.

But by February of the following year Jack Diamond was arrested and lay in Chichester Gaol. Whether he was there as a result of Chater's boasting and blabbing is unclear. After all, there was a reward of £500 on the head of each man who had broken into the Customs House, so perhaps this had led to Diamond's arrest.

Customs service officers now called on Chater. They had heard that he had spoken to Diamond at Fordingbridge in the company of the other smugglers, had been told that he had received a packet of the contraband tea. That being so, Chater was told, he was required to identify Diamond formally and then to swear before a magistrate that he had been carrying tea and had been armed. At some later time he might be required to appear in court as a witness.

Chater had not known that it might come to this. He had never been prepared for such an eventuality, to swear to the identity of a lawbreaker. He was aware of the possible consequences of giving information of this nature and we can imagine his reluctance to play the part asked of him. But what were the alternatives? He would be prosecuted, would himself be sent to gaol. He would be safe enough, Chater was reassured. He would have the backing of the law, he was told. He would be given some protection.

The laxness of those who wished to use Chater as a prosecution witness in a major case of organised crime is astonishing. Witness protection was paramount and past experience ought to have been enough to warn those responsible that Daniel Chater was in very real danger. As it was, Chater set out on the biting cold morning of Sunday 14 February, protected by one unarmed man, an equally aged minor customs official, William Galley, with no previous experience of protecting a witness. Perhaps had these two men, who were to meet such horrific deaths, taken care to plan their journey they might not have fallen into the clutches of such wicked people as they did. But they did not know their precise route and they strayed by chance across the paths of their murderers.

The plan was that they should travel to Stanstead and there hand over a document to Major William Battine, a magistrate and the Surveyor General of Customs for Sussex. But at Havant they were lost. Stanstead? In an age when few travelled far they probably asked directions several times and possibly received as many differing answers. But Rowland's Castle seemed a reasonable proposition and, wrapped up in their greatcoats, with an icy wind blowing, they made their miserable way northwards. At the New Inn at Leigh they stopped off for a drink to warm their bones.

Perhaps the warmth of the pub cheers their spirits, for Chater shows the important letter he is carrying to other customers. And Galley, perhaps not wishing to be outdone, may emphasise his significant role in looking after a man who is likely to be a star witness in an important forthcoming trial. But they cannot help chattering, either of them, and they bid farewell to their audience and continue on their cruel and bitter winter journey.

Sometime after midday it is time for another halt, for they have been on their way for several hours and are yet again chilled to the bone. At Rowland's Castle they stop off at the White Hart and call for a tot of rum. Would that they had never called here. Would that they had never bragged about their mission to the widow, Elizabeth Payne, who has the licence here. They talk and she listens, and then they tell her that it is time for them to be going. But no, she tells them, they cannot leave, not yet; their horses are in the stable and the ostler has just gone off with the key. He'll be back shortly, she says, so why not have another drink? What else can they do? So they charge their glasses once more. And as they drink and await the return of the ostler, more customers come in. They join the two travellers, have drinks with them, talk about this important business they are on. Then Galley senses something is wrong. He is unhappy, wonders if they aren't giving too much away, wonders if Chater is not talking just that bit too much. And why has the ostler not returned? One man, named Edmund Richards, has actually drawn a loaded pistol and pointed it at those drinking and said, 'Whoever discovers anything that passes at this house today, I will blow his brains out.' The other customers are now told to leave. What can this mean? But along comes the Widow Payne, telling them all to cheer up and have another drink.

Out in the yard where he has gone to relieve himself, Galley meets one of those who have been with them for the last hour or so. This is William Jackson of Westbourne. They have words. Galley says that he thinks that the witness is being

Galley (1) and Chater (2) are put on one horse by the gang of smugglers near Rowland's Castle.

interfered with and he pulls his warrant card out of his pocket. He is acting 'in the King's name', he says. He is a King's officer, he tells Jackson, and writes down his name in his note book. But Galley has no authority here. Perhaps he is already drunk. 'You a King's officer?' Jackson shouts at him. 'I'll make a King's officer of you. For a quartern of gin I'll serve you so again!'

Certainly an hour or so later both Galley and Chater are dead drunk and are carried off to bed. The letter that Chater has flourished so proudly is taken out of his pocket and destroyed.

Down in the taproom, those whom the Widow Payne so cunningly summoned earlier in the afternoon now discuss what they are to do with the two men asleep upstairs. They are dangerous company, smugglers all of them, and vicious too. William Jackson, the worst of characters, mistrusted even by those he works with, sits alongside Edmund Richards, 'a notorious wicked fellow'. And there is also 'Little Harry' Sheerman and William Carter, as well as 'Little Sam' Downer, William Steel and John Raiss. They are discussing desperate measures. They are agreed that these men cannot be allowed to live. They are at one in that. Yet, remember, an Act of Indemnity has been passed by the government. This Act makes smugglers vulnerable to informers. Anyone, any smuggler, even one in custody, could, if he named past accomplices, receive a pardon and a reward for all his past offences. The gang in the taproom know what their immediate intentions are but they do not know that, within the year, two of those around the table will name names, will betray the others sitting there.

Now all are agreed on everything but how to dispose of the two fellows sleeping off the afternoon's rum intake. Should they be instantly murdered? Steel suggested that they should get rid of them, and throw the bodies down a local well, but that proposal was rejected. It was too close to home, the others said. What about keeping them permanently locked up? But that was impractical. The wives of Jackson and Carter had turned up and felt at liberty to offer their own opinion on how the matter should be determined. 'Hang the dogs,' they urged the menfolk, 'for they came here to hang us.'

Eventually it was determined that they needed to be taken away from Rowland's Castle, as far away as possible. And so now, swathed in long mufflers and wearing heavy greatcoats, six of the group prepared their horses. Only John Raiss stayed behind as he had no horse.

Jackson and the others went to the room where Chater and Galley were still asleep. They were aroused by shouts, punches, whips cut into their backs. Jackson raised his topboot and drew his spur across the foreheads of both befuddled men. Still feeling the effects of the rum they drank earlier, the two wretched men stagger out of the bedroom, go down to the taproom and are pushed out into the freezing air of early evening. Blows still rain down on them. They are punched, the two old men; the heavy weighted ends of whip handles fall on their shoulders; they are kicked and cursed and sneered at. They are already bewildered and frightened, these two men who had set off as innocents that morning. No one says that they wept, but they assuredly did. There is no indication that they cried out for mercy, but there can be no doubt that they did.

Of course, their attackers are themselves drunk and they encourage each other in their brutality. Later, during the night, the effects of alcohol will wear off, but their ill-treatment will not lessen. They will continue throughout the long hours of the night and into the following two days to demonstrate not the least ounce of pity or human sympathy. What they perpetrate cannot be excused as the consequence of too much drink. At no point does it seem that anyone of this group had even a moment's reflection that what was happening was at the frontier of human cruelty.

Galley and Chater are placed up on one horse. Their ankles are tied under the horse's belly. And they are tied to each other by the legs. And off they set towards Finchdean, with Jackson's voice calling out almost as they leave the White Hart yard, 'Whip the dogs! Cut them, slash them, damn them!'

So they make a slow trail across the frost-hard roadway, the gang members taking it in turn to follow Jackson's injunction. And who can stop them? Who can even know what they do in this empty, wooded, winter-dark countryside? Who can call out at the sight of the terrified victims, whimpering, flinching, striving to escape the blows? What sorts of men are these who cannot feel the slightest pity? When they pass through Woodhouse Ashes, the shoemaker and the customs official fall from the horse's back and their captors now suspend them beneath the animal's belly. But then, tiring of this sport, they untie the two and then set them up once more on the horse's back and give them another beating for their pains. And Galley's coat, torn now from the blows from the whips, is taken off his back. He will feel the blows even more keenly now. But let him not call out in pain as they pass through Finchdean. Let him not dare. Neither of them must make a noise now, and the

The two men fall off their mount at Woodhouse Ashes.

pistols are out and levelled at them. And later they slip from the horse again, again find themselves upside down, their bound heels in the air, their heads trailing on the ground.

Now they are transferred. Galley is shoved up on to Steel's mount, sitting behind the rider, and Chater is similarly behind 'Little Sam'. But this does not save them. They are still beaten with the heavy whip handles. When they reach Lady Holt Park, Galley slips to the ground. In his pain the stricken man begs them to do away with him. He can bear this no longer. But they ignore his pleas and lift him up once more behind Steel. Yet again, as they cross Harting Down, he falls off the horse, and this time he is slung over Richards's horse, and held in place by Carter and Jackson. Galley pleads with them again. 'For God's sake, shoot me through the head,' he shouts. But his captors laugh and Jackson squeezes the old man's genitals.

It is past midnight now and they have trailed along these roads and lanes and downland paths for six hours. They have called at only one house, an old friend's place, where they ask if they can stay for a while, but he sizes up the matter, sees the two captives, divines what it is that they intend, and he turns them away.

Shortly after this, in Conduit Lane, Galley slips sideways on the horse, calling out that he is falling. 'Fall and be damned,' 'Little Harry' Sheerman tells him, and it may be that he pushes Galley so that he falls heavily. When they go once more to remount him they find that he is lifeless. So what now? The body is heaved up on to the horse's back and the party trudges on.

They make for Rake. Here, at the Red Lion, the owner, William Scardefield, very unwillingly lets them in. He sees Chater, 'whose face was a gore of blood, many of his teeth beat out, his eyes swelled and one almost destroyed', and what may be a corpse. They have been in a fight with customs men, Scardefield is told. Some of their men have been killed and others wounded. They explain that somehow they have taken a prisoner or a witness and Scardefield wonders what they intend to

The smugglers prepare to dig a hole in which to bury William Galley.

do with him. He fears the worst but agrees to allow them to put the man in a hut while Galley's body is hidden temporarily in the brewhouse. And after some time for further discussion and a drink, Galley's body is once more thrown across a horse. Scardefield leads the party to Harting Coombe, a mile away. Here, in woodland and by lantern light, the body is buried by Carter, Downer and Steel.

Then through the hours from dawn until late at night the gang sit drinking in the Red Lion, pondering their next move. From time to time they check that Chater is still in the hut but how can he not be? He is shackled to a post. That does not save him from their taunts, their threats, their kicks. They have not softened in their view of the helpless old man. Occasionally they give him food, but he vomits over himself, a hapless victim. Over the hours not one of the gang has considered if what they are doing can in any way be justified.

But Chater is a problem. Not their exclusive problem, the men tell themselves. After all Jack Diamond is a Chichester man and this whole business is about him. They have done their share, these Hampshire men, why not bring in the Sussex men? And so Jackson and 'Little Harry' Sheerman go off to Trotton with Chater in tow, still being beaten with whips across the face and neck as they go along. They have gone to seek out that old smuggling rogue, Richard Mills. He will understand the problem.

The Red Lion at Rake, drawn by C.G. Harper.

And he does. 'Major', for that is how he is known, locks the prisoner in a lean-to shed where normally he dries out turf for fuel. Here, on the freezing Monday night, Chater, exhausted and afraid, is placed on a pile of turf and chained to a beam. From time to time, 'Major' Mills comes in to taunt him as an informer, telling him that he will not live long. And 'Little Harry' and 'Little Sam' stand guard and add to the jeers and the blows.

Several of the gang returned to their homes in the course of the Tuesday, fearful perhaps that their absence might arouse suspicion, but on the next day they made their way back, this time with John Raiss, to the Red Lion, where they were to meet 'Major' and his acquaintances on the Wednesday evening. At this gathering were several Chichester men: John Cobby, William Hammond, Benjamin Tapner and Thomas Stringer; Daniel Perryer of Norton, 'Major' Mills and his sons, Richard and John, and, from Selborne, Thomas Willis. What should they do? How should they kill him? Should they load a gun and level it at Chater's head and then tie a piece of string to the trigger? Then they could all pull on the string together. That would make them equally guilty. They would not then

Daniel Chater in chains.

inform on each other. But that would mean the game was over, and there is no doubt that they were enjoying the game, the suffering, the power. At least it was agreed that the Sussex men should have the responsibility for getting rid of Chater. 'We have done our parts and you shall do yours,' Jackson told them. It was decided that Chater should be thrown down Harris's Well at Lady Holt Park. After all, the well was dry and never used. The body could lie there for ever and no one would ever suspect that a corpse lay there.

The gang returned to Trotton, where Chater lay in the lean-to. Tapner lunged forward with his clasp-knife and cut him across the eyes and nose 'so that he almost cut both his eyes out and the gristle of his nose quite through'. But that was not enough for Tapner, who then slashed him across the forehead. 'This knife shall be his butcher,' he shouted, but 'Major' Mills was rather more cautious. It was his house, after all. 'Pray don't murder him here. Carry him somewhere else before you do it.'

At the well, after another ride in the dark, Tapner placed a short cord round Chater's neck. No long drop for him, no sharp, sudden breaking of the neck. He would strangle slowly. Then he was made to clamber over the protective fence and pushed to the edge of the well. The rope was tied to the fence and the desperate old man was pushed over, though, because of the shortness of the rope only his legs dangled in the well. And for the next quarter of an hour, half-sitting, half-standing, he choked. And then, before he died, the rope was taken from his neck and he was suspended by the ankles, held upside down over the well by Stringer, Cobby and Hammond. Then, at last, they let him go, head first. Even so, the wretched, still fearful old man did not immediately die. They could hear him sobbing and groaning at the bottom of the well. They threw down two wooden gate-posts and then large flints. Eventually they silenced him. Chater's suffering had lasted from the Sunday afternoon until the early hours of Thursday.

For several months after, no one knew what had happened to either of the two missing men. There might well have been strong suspicions, but as to who was responsible for their disappearance there was not the slightest hint. The gang must have felt very safe, for who would dare to report them? As for the prosecution of Diamond, without the vital witness how could it be expected to prosper? Even the offer of further reward failed to produce the merest whisper until, quite out of the blue, there came an anonymous letter. Addressed to 'a person of distinction', it

Chater is suspended over the well.

The smugglers hurl stones down the well in which they have thrown Chater.

purported to come from 'one of the persons who had been a witness to some of the transactions of this bloody tragedy, though he was no way concerned in the murder'. It remains unknown who wrote the letter, but it contained vital information as to Galley's burial place. There is, however, an alternative account that Galley's body was found by chance by a gentleman out hunting.

The body was found buried in an almost standing position, still wearing boots, gloves, waistcoat and breeches. What struck those who dug it up was that the hands appeared to be covering the eyes. There were suggestions that Galley had not been dead when he was put in the ground. Rather, it was thought that he had been deeply unconscious when he was buried and that later, under the ground, he had come to and had made some effort to struggle from his grave.

Then in September 1748 came another whisper, another breakthrough, leading this time to William Steel. Just a reminder: this is the William Steel who on the Sunday afternoon at the White Hart had unsuccessfully proposed getting rid of Chater and Galley straightaway by killing them and dropping them down a well; the same Steel present at all of the discussions at the Red Lion and at Mills's house at Trotton; the same man who with two others buried Galley's tortured frame. And,

Galley is placed in his grave.

taken into custody, he recalled the Act of Indemnity and offered at once to tell the authorities what had happened and who exactly had been involved.

Then John Raiss came forward. One of the Hampshire men, he had played little part in the murder of Galley, but he had played a significant role in the murder of Chater.

He too offered the authorities all the help he could.

Now Chater's body was retrieved from the well. 'The body was found with a rope about his neck, his eyes appeared to have been cut or picked out of his head . . . They got his body out of the well with only one leg on.'

By October William Hammond and John Cobby were lodged in Horsham Gaol, and the following month Benjamin Tapner was placed under arrest; he too was charged with murder. Over the months others, including the two most vicious torturers, Jackson and Carter, were arrested.

On 17 January 1749, at a Special Assize at Chichester, Mr Justice Foster handed down sentences of death on the seven men standing in leg irons in the dock: Tapner, Cobby and Hammond were named as principals in the murder of Daniel Chater; William Jackson and William Carter as principals in the murder of William Galley.

These men were sentenced to be hanged and later gibbeted. Richard Mills the Elder and his son, Richard Mills the Younger, were to suffer hanging but were not to be gibbeted.

They were to be executed the next day and so, on their return to gaol from court, five of them were measured for the suits of chains and straps that they would wear on the gibbet after their corpses had been tarred. Within two hours Jackson was dead, as a consequence, it is said, of fright.

At two o'clock on the afternoon of 18 January, with Guards and Dragoons in attendance, the six men due to hang were marched through Chichester and up the Midhurst Road to The Broyle. They climbed up on to a long wagon placed under the gallows which had cost £42 to erect, a sum that the Corporation of Chichester would ultimately recover from the Exchequer.

Tapner, Hammond, Cobby and Carter took the opportunity to address the dense crowd, forgiving everyone, even the informants. 'Major' Mills and his son were less forgiving, refusing even at this stage to accept that they were guilty.

A letter from a Chichester correspondent, dated 20 January 1749, describes the occasion. 'Young Mills talk't very narrowly and said we shall have a very jolly Hang of it and at the place of execution he said it was very hard to be refused a pint of beer which he had asked for. The father would have smok'd from the Gaol to the gallows but was prevented.'

The writer goes on to complain that the executioner was not sufficiently expert and produced ropes that were too short. Others had to be sent for, which meant an hour's delay. 'Young Mills', says the correspondent, 'amused himself most of the time in looking up at the executioner who sat across the gallows, and smiled several times as is supposed at the hangman's going so awkwardly about his work. Tapner and Carter were very devout and gave a great deal of good advice to the spectators, the former recommended in a very strong manner to the Dragoons and soldiers who attended the execution to be very vigilant in their endeavours to take one Richards who he said was one of the worst of the gang and the principal cause of his coming to so shameful an end.'

'Major' Mills, defiant to the last, had to stand on tiptoe as the rope went round his neck. It was still too short. 'Don't hang me by inches,' he called out. Perhaps he remembered poor Chater's end.

And finally the horse was driven away and the six murderers were left to dance 'the hempen jig'.

Carter's body was placed on the gibbet at Rake; Chapman's at Rook's Hill near Chichester; Cobby's and Hammond's corpses were sited near Selsey Bill. The bodies of the two Millses, along with Jackson's, were flung into a hole near the gallows.

And the others? 'Little Harry' Sheerman was hanged after East Grinstead Assizes some months later and he too was gibbeted at Rake. At the same Assizes John Mills, son of 'Major', was found guilty of a brutal murder and hanged on Slindon Common. He was the third member of his family to be executed in three months.

Edmund Richards, one of Galley's murderers, was hanged at Lewes in July 1749 and gibbeted on Hambrook Common.

Thanks to the further testimony of Steel and Raiss, ten men, including Richard Perrin, William Fairall and Thomas Kingsmill, the leading lights in the Poole Customs House raid, and one woman, were sentenced to death in April 1749. And it was this matter at Poole which had in the first place led to the horrific murders of two decent old men. These murders resulted in such a wave of revulsion that not only were the murderers brought to book but the smuggling fraternity received a blow from which it never quite recovered. Though smuggling would continue in great volume, never again would smugglers threaten the rule of law.

2

SALLY CHURCHMAN'S 'SNUFF'

Broadbridge Heath, 1751

Poor James Whale, a thirty-or-so-year-old labourer, just another young death in an age when such a short life was not remarkable. Horsham parish church burial register records his passing somewhat starkly: '1751 October 13th, James Wale [*sic*], a poor man.' It does not record that he left a wife, Anne, only twenty years of age, and a year-old child. How would they now manage? Would it be the workhouse? A life of meagre hand-outs from the parish overseers? After all, her husband had been, as the register stated, 'poor'. Oddly enough, neither of these prospects was likely, for when she reached twenty-one, Anne was due to inherit £80 from an uncle.

If there were any doubts about the circumstances of James Whale's death, these were soon proved to be groundless.

An inquisition indented and taken at the town of Horsham in the said county the thirty first day of October and from thence continued and adjourned to the first day of November in the twenty-fifth year of the reign of our Sovereign Lord George II before Thomas Attree, Esquire, coroner, and a jury of fourteen good and lawful men of the Burrough and town of Horsham who say and present upon their oath that on Thursday the tenth day of October about the hour of eight o'clock in the forenoon, James Whale in his own dwelling house in Horsham aforesaid was found dead; that upon their view of the body of the said James Whale no marks of violence appearing thereon or any fracture contusion or wound which might occasion his death, the jurors upon their oath say that the said James Whale by the visitation of Almighty God and not otherwise, came by his death.

Perhaps the inquest caused Anne some anxieties, as well it might for she had after all murdered her husband. But once that 'visitation of Almighty God' had been declared she doubtless felt a load lifted. Perhaps she intended returning to the roistering, boisterous, carefree life that she had once enjoyed. She had had enough of the rather staid man her mother had persuaded her to marry. And she had some money. Life would be different now that she was free. But Anne Whale would be dead before another twelve months had passed, unable to pursue the pleasures of the past.

How had it come to this pass? It was not as if life had ever been hard or brutal, not as if she had been born into a criminal family. She was the daughter, one of several children, of highly respectable parents, well known in Horsham where her father, William Waterton, was a butcher. They lived happily – there is no reason to think otherwise – at The Cock Inn on The Carfax. Girls of her upbringing and education were usually described as 'genteel'. But this description did not fit Anne. Once her father died her mother was unable to keep her under control. She was wilful, disobedient and as she grew into young womanhood she showed less and less inclination to behave with any kind of moderation. For a while she left home, mixing with all kinds of dubious characters, and why she suddenly decided to reform herself and settle down at the age of eighteen is not known. But she seems to have made some resolution to mend her ways and returned home to her mother.

What is astonishing is that in double-quick time, in 1749, the eighteen-year-old Anne was married to James Whale. She seems to have put up no resistance to her mother's suggestion that though he was only a labourer he was the right man for her. He was sober, reliable, steady, possessed of all those virtues that a mother might see as desirable in a son-in-law. Within ten days of meeting James, Anne was married. Ten days is rather a brief time for a courtship, but in this case the mother, desperate to find someone who would keep her daughter from her past follies, urged the match.

So, married, off they moved, first to Steepwood in West Chiltington and then to Pulborough. But in August 1750 they arrived at Corsletts in Broadbridge Heath, renting from Mr John Agate part of a farmhouse cottage where Anne's cousin, Sarah Pledge, was already installed with her husband, another James, and seven children. It was an unholy alliance, this reunion of cousins. Older than Anne, Sarah might have been expected to be rather more sober and mature, someone who might restrain the wilful younger cousin. But it is as if Anne deliberately sought out Sarah as someone as reckless and unreliable as herself. Perhaps had James Whale been aware of Sarah's disposition beforehand, he might never have moved to Corsletts. He had nothing in common with the loud, coarse Sarah Pledge, nor her untrustworthy husband.

James Whale's stay at Corsletts must have been deeply unhappy. He fell out with the Pledges, at one time barring Sarah from the rooms in his part of the house. He tried to forbid Anne to talk to Sarah, convinced that she was a bad influence. It must have been an embarrassing situation, living so close together in an atmosphere of mutual dislike and hostility. And where Anne stood in all of this is very obvious. She sided with her cousin, that ill-natured woman, who very evidently encouraged the growing rift between the young couple. Whale's disapproval of his wife's relatives must increasingly have soured the marriage. Was there something here connected with the money Anne was shortly due to inherit? Was her husband fearful that under the influence of the Pledges she would squander it? Was Anne resentful that her husband wanted her to be prudent with the cash which even then was a useful sum though not a princely fortune? By today's reckoning, £80 would be worth £10,000, a very decent windfall but one which could be frittered away by fecklessness. James Whale knew of his wife's past, knew that she could take no heed of the morrow, and perhaps he also felt that the Pledges would encourage her to spend more than she ought to. So was James regularly counselling his wife to be thrifty and particularly not to trust Sarah and her husband? If he was, would this not irritate the young wife, make her wish she had never been married to such a dull dog, yearn more than anything for the freedom that she now regretted having lost?

This difficult situation continued over the months, the two women closer than ever, constantly in each other's company, increasingly impatient with Whale. Around harvest time of 1751 one of the women broached a solution. Was it Anne? Or Sarah? Impossible to say, but out of their daily frustrations with James Whale they were gradually able to hint to each other at how things might be resolved. Perhaps for weeks they had skirted around the possibility, not wishing to come out with the awful proposal, not daring to voice outright what they had been working towards.

In her confession, Anne was to describe Sarah's bold decision. At last she had come to the point.

'Nan, I say, let us get rid of this devil,' Sarah says.

Out at last, the unutterable uttered. And Anne doesn't recoil in horror, doesn't disown her cousin.

'How?' is what she says. She is all for ridding herself of her husband.

And Sarah has no hesitation. She has thought this out, knows what can be done.

'With some poison,' she replies.

And poison is easy enough come by. Any little village shop will sell you arsenic, the king of poisons. Just tell them you have mice or rats and no questions are asked. But Sarah has some in the house already, she tells her cousin. Then, when she goes to look, she cannot find it. So she goes off to Horsham full of enthusiasm for the task. But at the apothecary's door she looks at Mr Harfoy and thinks that he might remember her should anything go wrong. After all, it's such a small place, only 2,000 inhabitants. Everybody knows everybody. So then she goes over to Rusper but has the same frisson as soon as she steps inside the shop, and returns once more empty-handed to Broadbridge Heath. And it's the same when she goes to Dorking.

One day, perhaps frustrated at the progress of the plan, Anne asks if Sarah's husband knows anything about poisoning.

'Go and talk to him yourself,' Sarah tells her.

'What shall I do to get rid of my cross devil?' Anne asks James Pledge.

'I'll tell you how,' Pledge answers. 'Get a pennyworth of poison which is called arsenic. It is very much like loaf sugar. Put it into some tea or some beer, sweeten it well and he won't taste it for it has no taste at all, for I have tasted it. It is only a little brackish.'

'And if I do it, how shall I keep my child and pay such a large rent?' This leaves another question hanging: what about the inheritance?

Pledge says that she can live with them rent free as long as she is a widow, which further convinces Anne that she should proceed in her purpose.

A
GENUINE ACCOUNT

OF

ANNE WHALE and SARAH PLEDGE,

Who were tried and condemned at the Affizes held at *Horſham* in the County of *Suſſex*,

Before the Right Honble Sir JOHN WILLES, Lord Chief Juſtice of his Majeſty's Court of *Common Pleas*,

AND

Sir THOMAS DENISON, K^nt, one of his Majeſty's Juſtices, the 20th of *July*, 1752.

For the barbarous and inhuman Murder of JAMES WHALE, Husband of the ſaid ANNE WHALE, by Poiſon, when ANNE WHALE was ſentenced to be burnt, in being guilty of Petty Treaſon.

And SARAH PLEDGE to be hanged, as being an Acceſſary, Aider and Abettor in the ſaid Crime, which Sentence was accordingly executed on them on *Friday* the 7th of *Auguſt* 1752, at *Horſham* aforeſaid.

Together with their Authentick Examinations and Confeſſions, taken before JOHN WICKER, and SAMUEL BLUNT, Eſqrs, two of his Majeſty's Juſtices of the Peace for the County of *Suſſex*.

This Pamphlet is worthy the Peruſal of Perſons of all Ranks and Denominations, as it contains a Series of uncommon Events, and more particularly the remarkable Contrivance of *Sarah Pledge*, in endeavouring to poiſon the ſaid *James Whale*, by putting Spiders in his Beer.

L O N D O N:

Printed for M. COOPER, at the *Globe* in *Pater-noſter Row*, and Meſſrs. VERRAL and LEE, at *Lewes*.

[Price Six-Pence.]

Front cover of a pamphlet purporting to tell the true story of Anne Whale and Sarah Pledge.

Anne's statement says that James Pledge also went three times to town to get poison but was afraid to buy it because he thought she might renege and denounce him.

Desperate measures are needed if they are to carry out what they have talked about for so long. And Sarah remembers an old folk poison. She goes to the granary and collects spiders, which she puts in a cup.

'Good God! What you did you get them for?' Anne asks her when she takes them to her.

'They are pretty little birds to do for the Prince,' Sarah tells her. She says she is going to pour beer over them and then she will bake them. Then, after they are baked and are hard and dry and black, she will take them between finger and thumb and squeeze them, and this she will put into a bottle of beer. And when the Prince, as she calls him, drinks it, all will be over and it will look like a normal death. Nobody will ever suspect.

It is not a very complicated or time-consuming task to bake a few spiders, and Sarah soon has the potion ready for Anne in a beer bottle. It is left on the table for James's supper.

But Anne Whale's statement now surprises us, for she says that she takes the bottle and throws it into a ditch. Why? Has she changed her mind? Or is she hoping that she can cast some of the blame on Sarah? In any event, when Sarah comes back to see her, hoping for news, hoping that James is already dead, she finds him hale and hearty. What has happened, Sarah asks? Anne has not the heart to tell her how she had disposed of the bottle. She says that James has not even been sick.

'Damn him,' Sarah says, like some wicked fairy-tale character. 'He has a constitution as strong as the devil. But the next dose I get for him shall be strong enough.' And off she goes to Mr Harfoy's shop at Horsham once again. There has been too much talk, too much shilly-shallying. This time she buys a pennyworth of arsenic. It is not all that difficult. She has rats, she tells Mr Harfoy. She needs to get rid of them.

At breakfast time the following morning, after Whale had left for work, Sarah went to see Anne. She handed her the packet of poison. When she looked at it, Anne could not believe the powder to be poison. Surely it was salts, she said to Sarah.

'By God, it is poison and it is that that shall do for your husband.' After all the trouble she had gone to, here was Anne doubting her!

'Why, you won't do it, will you?' Anne asks her. She is hesitant now, dubious about what they are up to, unable to do the deed when it comes to the pinch. Or so she said; this is taken from the confession to her hideous, monstrous crime and she needs somehow to take some of the responsibility off her young shoulders.

'Yes, by God, I will if you will not,' Sarah answers.

And Anne has even more reservations. 'If we do it we shall be all took up and hanged,' she says.

But Sarah urges her on. 'No, it will never be found out if you don't tell but, by God, you shall have a hand in it or else you will tell.'

Sarah thinks she needs some kind of insurance and she will not do it alone. But there is really nothing to fear, she tells her cousin. She has done something like this before, she says, and has got away with it.

Sarah is so keen that it is difficult to assess the reason for such enthusiasm. Can it really be the promise of a share in Anne's inheritance? Anyway, she knows how the poison can be administered. Anne will make a hasty pudding for James's dinner the next day.

The next day, Wednesday 9 October, James has come home from work and perhaps is looking forward to the hasty pudding, one of his favourites. He plays with the baby while the meal is prepared. And Sarah just pops in – he has not put a stop to their talking together – and hands Anne a roll of paper. 'Here's the snuff Sally Churchman has sent to you.' Anne thanks her for the 'snuff' and Sarah goes back home. Anne busies herself mixing the flour and milk, the butter and sugar and eggs. It is a quick enough dish to make, as its name suggests. Soon it is ready and she upturns the pot in which it has been cooked and out it comes. James is too busy with the child to see Anne sprinkle the powder into the bottom of the pan. When it comes to serving she takes the top part of the pudding. She may even give a spoonful or so to the baby. But the greater portion is for her husband, who has been hard at work all day. He gets the bottom of the pot and presumably he enjoys it, scraping away every last morsel.

In the course of the evening Whale was sick, though not ill enough to prevent him going out to see his landlord, Mr Agate. He had paid the rent and had gone to seek a receipt. On the way back, however, and just as he reached home, he was seen leaning over the fence being violently sick. He staggered home and went straight upstairs to bed. Anne went to the Pledges, ostensibly for a warming pan but more likely to report progress.

The following day Anne called on two male neighbours to help her lift her husband back into bed. He had been seriously ill all night and was on the point of death. He must have eaten a considerable quantity of arsenic for it to have had such an immediate and drastic effect upon him. By eight o'clock that evening he was dead.

And then, within a fortnight, the exhumation, followed by the coroner's jury's verdict, attributing his sudden death to 'a visitation by Almighty God'. From now everything must have seemed right for the two women.

Then, months later, in the late spring, Mr Agate, the landlord at Corsletts, had occasion to visit Mr Harfoy, the Horsham apothecary. In the course of a brief over-the-counter conversation, Harfoy happened to ask Agate about the rats. The rats? What rats? Had Agate heard aright? What did Mr Harfoy mean by his remark? The rats that they'd been having trouble with last year, the ones Mrs Pledge had come in about, the ones she'd bought a pennyworth of poison for. The query bemused Agate. Perhaps he had forgotten. Or possibly Mrs Pledge had taken it upon herself to try to cure a problem. Perhaps she hadn't wished to bother him for a penny which was all she had spent. Or perhaps . . .

The more he thought about his conversation with the apothecary, the more concerned Harfoy became. After all, James Whale's end had been so sudden, so unexpected. Had his death been 'occasioned by some sinister arts'? It was worrying enough for Agate to seek advice from a magistrate.

Whether there was a second exhumation is not known, though it is unlikely. After all, if poison was suspected, no doctor had knowledge enough to analyse a victim's organs to prove the use of poison. Only months before, in March, the Blandy poisoning trial at Henley was the first at which medical evidence was called in relation to the cause of death but, even there, although Mary Blandy was found guilty, the doctor produced no scientific evidence. So the conclusion must be that the case at Horsham was conducted on what the two women under examination had told the magistrates.

Much of Anne's confession, dated and signed 6 July 1752, has formed the background to this account so far. But it is only fair to include some elements of Sarah Pledge's version. Just as Anne cast much of the blame on her cousin, so did Sarah blame Anne in her earlier confession of 3 May which she signed with her mark. There is no explanation of why there was such a gap between the writing of the two confessions, but the two women were arrested and imprisoned at the same time.

Sarah claimed that Anne had approached her as late as 7 October about getting rid of her husband. Anne had told her that if Sarah would buy her a pennyworth of poison, she would give her half a guinea to buy a new gown. In addition, Anne had said that if she was caught and hanged she would leave Sarah £10 to look after her child. It was a small recompense.

Both women were indicted at the Assizes, as was James Pledge, the charge in his case stating 'that he did feloniously and maliciously command and counsel the said Anne Whale to commit the said treason felony'.

Remarkably, for on the face of it he appears as guilty as the two women, he was discharged. There followed a one-day trial with an inevitable conclusion. Anne and Sarah had effectively condemned each other in their statements.

And so the trial came to its expected conclusion. 'Anne Whale and Sarah Pledge were indicted at the Assizes at Horsham on 20 July 1752 for the murder of James Whale, husband of the said Anne, and being convicted upon the clearest evidence were sentenced to death.'

Public execution of a woman for petty treason.

Their punishments were not identical. In the case of Sarah Pledge, the judge pronounced, 'Let her be hanged by the neck till she be dead, on Friday 24th July, and let her body be dissected and anatomised.'

For Anne was reserved the old punishment for petty treason, the murder of a husband, the great betrayal. 'Let her be taken from the jail and thence to be drawn upon a hurdle to the place of execution and there to be burned with fire till she be dead on Friday 24th July.'

The pair were respited until 7 August, during which time they behaved in a quite contrasting fashion. Anne Whale, it appears, was resigned to her fate but her cousin adopted 'a most hardened manner, making use of profane expressions, and declaring that she would fight the hangman at the place of execution'. Told that her clothing was part of the hangman's perks, she declared that she 'would sooner chuse to be hanged naked than that he should have any of her cloathes'. As for Anne, whom she now believed was responsible for her present misfortune, she hoped 'to see the young bitch burnt before she herself was hanged'.

On the evening before their execution both women received the sacrament and were said to have forgiven each other. On her last morning, Sarah spoke to her husband and one of her children followed her to the gallows.

The executions took place on Broadbridge Heath common. Sarah was taken by cart, as was usual. At half past three she was hanged. Her screams as she stood under the rope, so it was said, could be heard two miles away.

Two hours later Anne was chained to the stake. An account written at the time tells the rest:

> The parson prayed for and with her for upwards of half an hour before she was strangled. This was about five minutes before the fire was kindled, which was one of the greatest ever known upon such a melancholy occasion. There were upwards of three hundred and one half of faggots and three loads of cordwood so that it must have continued burning till Saturday night or Sunday morning. The faggots eclipsed the sight of her for some time, but in about five minutes the violence of the flames consumed a part thereof which falling gave the spectators an opportunity of seeing her – a very affecting and disagreeable object, for she was all consumed to a skeleton. She said nothing at the place of execution – the whole ceremony was carried on with the strictest decorum and decency and there was the biggest concourse of people ever known on a like occasion. The body of Sarah Pledge was put into a tallow chandler's hamper and carried to Dr Dennet, junior, of Storrington, to be dissected agreeable to the late Act of Parliament.

In Broadbridge Heath. All of this. Bloody murder by two mothers. The public spectacle of a hanging and a burning. Ordinary places. Ordinary people, you might think. A shade wayward, perhaps. But would anyone ever have suspected how things would turn out?

3

THE BODY IN GLADISH WOOD

Burwash, 1826

In the early years of the nineteenth century the Burwash district, now always so green, so rich, so well tended, was markedly different. Its inhabitants, not unlike so many throughout the country, were sunk in a deep and wretched poverty. It was a harsh and bitter time.

Men, many of them without regular work, were employed by the Burwash Vestry as road-menders, and were at their often back-breaking tasks from half past six in the morning until six o'clock at night. And woe betide the man who turned up late, for his meagre allowance would be docked, and let him not dare to take home any wood, tree branches and the like, which did not belong to him. As for the children of the poor, in this sad time, some were sent to the poorhouse, away from the squalid cottages occupied by their starving parents. But even the very poor, who might have been excused for thinking that their fortunes could not have sunk any further, might have been surprised in 1825 at the decision of the Vestry, which possessed even more powers than a modern local council, when it 'Resolved that all Allowances of Flour be taken off from Paupers who have less than five children.' Such random illustrations as these may be enough to explain, if not to excuse, why crime was endemic. Not that similar conditions did not prevail throughout the country.

In the Burwash area there was always the menace of footpads, sometimes armed, though so ferocious and threatening were many of them that they needed neither guns nor knives nor cudgels to frighten their victims into handing over their money or their property. There were experienced groups of burglars in the neighbourhood as well as barn robbers, poachers and scores of smugglers. None of these law-breakers was hindered by the merest hint of a police force, the faintest idea of which was vehemently opposed as un-English though the principal fear was that their introduction would cause the rates to rise. And it was against this depressed and lawless background that an unexpected death occurred.

It is no surprise to learn that in these small rural backwaters there were people regularly on the move at night. Many of those who had dishonest business to conduct needed the cover of darkness. And under cover of darkness strange things happen. On one occasion a young man died.

The Wheel, Burwash Weald, c. 1890.

The *Sussex Advertiser* of 15 May 1826 gives the earliest report of the matter. 'Last Monday, a labouring man named Russell was found lying dead in a wood, nigh to Burwash. He had left his home the same morning, apparently in good health. An inquisition [inquest] has been since held on view of the body, which we understand, for the satisfaction of the jury, was opened; some circumstances having appeared which led to the suspicion that the deceased had swallowed arsenic.'

The verdict was that Benjamin Russell 'died by poison, but whether taken by the deceased intentionally, or administered by another, the jury could not ascertain'. At the post-mortem, according to the local surgeon, Mr Evans, nearly a drachm of arsenic had been found in the dead man's stomach.

Thirty-five-year-old Russell and his wife Hannah ran The Wheel, a notorious public house at Burwash Weald, spoken of by some at the time as one of the roughest pubs in the south-east. As soon as the body was found, even before the autopsy, rumours of murder had run round the parish and beyond. Whispering voices had already identified those responsible. Ben Russell was the victim of his wife and her young lover, Daniel Leany.

It was also easy to understand. The newspapers were to write of the 31-year-old Hannah speaking of Daniel 'in terms of gross affection'. For weeks, she had conducted a very open affair with her nineteen-year-old lodger. Whether her husband was aware of what was going on is unclear, but many of the inhabitants of Burwash knew of the liaison. Within days, after the magistrates had been presented with the medical evidence, they charged the dead man's wife and her lover with murder. They were arrested and taken to Horsham gaol to await their trial at the Summer Assizes in Lewes.

The feelings of many of the more conservative people in Burwash, outraged at what had occurred, were summed up at a Vestry meeting held only three weeks before the case came to trial.

At a General Meeting of the Inhabitants of this Parish in Vestry assembled this fifth day of July 1826 (Public Notice having been first given) for the purpose of taking into consideration the prosecution of Hannah Russell and Daniel Leany in the case of Ben Russell when it was Resolved unanimously that Mr Baldock be appointed as Chairman at the Meeting, when a motion was made to know whether the Parish of Burwash will pay all reasonable expenses (over and above what may be obtained from the County) in the prosecution of Hannah Russell and Daniel Leany.

The foregoing Motion was carried by a majority of 32 to 3.

It was obvious that Burwash had already made up its mind about what verdict it expected. The influence of the Russell family is felt here. This family, some of them edging into the middle class, had disapproved of Ben's marriage to Hannah and after his death they helped orchestrate the Vestry decision. The most powerful of the family was Frank Russell, a wealthy farmer, who had installed his nephew Ben at The Wheel, which he owned. He was a significant member of the Vestry, often chairing its meetings. That much of his money had been made through smuggling – and, some say, through dealing in stolen goods – did not deter him from pursuing those he believed had murdered his nephew.

The trial took place in the tiny crowded courtroom at Lewes on Friday 28 July, before Mr Baron Graham. It lasted twelve hours. Hannah Russell was indicted 'for wilfully, feloniously, and traitorously, and of her malice aforethought' murdering her husband. Daniel Leany was charged with 'feloniously aiding and assisting in the murder'.

With a candour typical of its time, *The Times* observed: 'The female prisoner, who appeared to be about 40 years of age, was, in fact, only 31; and the man, who appeared to be about 30, was in reality but 19. Both were persons of ill-favoured aspect, and in the lowest condition of life.' Another press report describes Hannah as a woman of 'rather forbidding aspect'.

For the prosecution, Mr Andrews said that his case depended solely upon circumstantial evidence but, he assured the jury, which included a number of Burwash men, that during the time he had practised at the bar, and for long before, judges had always declared this sort of evidence to be the best and most satisfactory. It was, after all, extremely difficult to forge a consistent chain of circumstances but, said Mr Andrews, he would prove that Hannah had on more than one occasion threatened to do away with her husband. He would prove that poison had been purchased and that Daniel Leany had given contradictory accounts of his movements on the night.

In all, the prosecution called twenty-two witnesses, six of them repeating threats they had heard Hannah make about her husband. Whether she had a genuine grievance is impossible to say, but it has been suggested that too much of Ben's time was spent away from The Wheel, attending fairs and prize-fights. At one point it was suggested by Hannah that her husband had other women friends.

The trial opened with Ben Russell's father relating how at about one o'clock on the morning of Monday 8 May he had been roused from his bed by the rattle of soil thrown against his window. Peering out, he had seen Leany and his daughter-in-law, Hannah. There was obviously some emergency and he went downstairs and let them in.

Ben was dead, they told William Russell. He had died over towards Brightling and they wanted help to carry him home. Leany explained that some hours earlier he and Ben had set off from The Wheel to steal wheat from a barn belonging to a Farmer Holloway in Brightling parish. They knew the district well enough and had without difficulty negotiated the rutted roads, had climbed fences and had walked through copses. They had successfully broken into the barn and had helped themselves to two sacks of wheat.

On their way back Ben had been carrying the heavier of the sacks but after only a hundred yards or so he complained of chest pains. He had refused Daniel's offer to exchange their loads and had walked on with the sack on his back. In the dark, the two men had become separated and shortly afterwards, when Daniel went to look for him, he had found his companion lying lifeless on the ground.

Daniel had gone back to The Wheel to tell Hannah what had happened and they agreed to seek William Russell's help. Now they intended to carry him home.

After the distressed William had dressed, he and Daniel walked the three miles to where the body had been left lying near Holloway's farmhouse. Ben, cold and stiff, lay on his back, his arms stretched out, by the side of the footpath.

William Russell told the court what happened next. On the walk over to Brightling, he had been giving the matter some thought and had persuaded Daniel that they should not try to carry Ben back to The Wheel. More or less on the spot they concocted a story that Ben had gone out alone to meet a man about a tub of smuggled spirits. If necessary, they would say that Daniel had arranged to follow and join him later to carry the tub back to The Wheel. Russell did not wish his son to be branded a common thief, a barn-breaker. This would be too shameful, too much for the family to bear. Smugglers, despite their dreadful crimes, were never regarded with the same degree of disapproval as common thieves because they were still considered to be performing a public service. Because of Russell's desire to save his family such shame, he now carried the body, with Daniel, four hundred yards into Gladish Wood where they left it lying among brambles and stubble. The abandoned wheat sacks they hid in a nearby field.

This part of the story is rather difficult to come to terms with. What has never been satisfactorily explained is whether at this stage William agreed to keep Daniel's name out of the equation when the body was found and enquiries were made. It was only as events were to unfold, when the couple were charged with murder, that William was prepared to say that his son did not go out alone to Gladish Wood.

And most important, at about four o'clock, Russell and Daniel had met a man called Hawkins near the wood. It was a most significant encounter. They must have hoped that he would remain silent about seeing them. After all, he himself might have been on some or other dishonest enterprise. But was that not too much to hope for? Within hours of hearing of Ben's death, Thomas Hawkins was chattering.

Frank Russell and Ben's brother appeared in the box, saying that there were inconsistencies in Daniel's accounts of the time at which he said he had found the body. Another witness, John Woodsell, told how he was in Gladish Wood at about eight o'clock on the Monday and saw Daniel Leany. Fifteen minutes or so later, Daniel had approached him. He said that he had found Ben Russell's body at the top of Gladish Wood. Woodsell said that Daniel told him that he had gone there expecting to meet Ben with a tub of gin at eight o'clock.

Some time after that, John Sheather had met Daniel leaving the wood. Daniel told him about finding Ben's body and had said that he was going back to Burwash Weald to tell Hannah.

In the afternoon Sheather had met Daniel again and asked him how he thought Hannah would cope now that she was widowed. Would she carry on at The Wheel? Would she be able to manage? Of course she would carry on, Daniel had told him. And he would be there to help. After all, he could get gin and beer as well as Ben had done. It was as if he was already prepared to assume a new role in the household.

Robert Bowles, the Burwash blacksmith, was another to take the witness stand. He said that he had called in at The Wheel at about seven o'clock on the Monday morning. Daniel had come in some time later, but not a word had been said about

The Wheel Inn, 2005. (Alan Skinner)

Ben, although he had now been dead for several hours. In conversation Hannah told Bowles that she had been very much alarmed earlier that morning. There had been a loud, 'blundering' noise upstairs. It was as if somebody had jumped out of bed. But there was only Mary, the baby, up there, and when Hannah went to find out what the noise was she found the baby still asleep and everything in its place. Was it an omen, she had wondered, for unexplained noises of that kind often betokened a death. She told Bowles that she hoped nothing had happened to her husband; maybe some relative had died. But she knew already what had happened.

Hannah also told Bowles that her husband had gone out early, between four and five o'clock. He had been to collect a tub of spirits. Daniel had gone to join him about half an hour later. The smuggling story, made up only after Ben's death, was well rooted in the early hours of the morning.

Later in the day, when Bowles heard about Ben's death, he went round to The Wheel again, presumably to express his regrets. He found Daniel and Hannah sitting together in front of the fireplace. Daniel told him how he had found the body and said that he had tried to lift Ben up and heard a gurgling noise in his throat. But was he sure that the man was dead? Bowles asked him. Mightn't he have just fallen down in a fit? But Daniel was adamant. When he had found the fallen man, he was dead.

That same Monday morning, at about ten o'clock, Elizabeth Elliott met Daniel going towards The Wheel. Was there a hint of a standing joke about the relationship between Hannah and Daniel when she made her light-hearted remark? 'I asked him how his mistress's temper was.'

He told her he did not know, 'but it would be worse when he got home . . . he had just been and found her old man dead.' And then Mrs Elliott too was served up the tale of the tub of spirits.

It seems that several people when they spoke to Hannah did so not simply to express their regrets at her husband's death. Some quite clearly, almost within hours of hearing of Ben's death, had made up their minds that something odd had taken place. Ananias Hilder, a labourer, for example thought that Hannah gave him inconsistent and contradictory accounts of several circumstances. He was certainly not reluctant to ask some very pressing questions at a time when perhaps he might have been respectfully quiet towards the widow. But not so.

What time had Daniel gone to bed on the Sunday night, he had asked her.

She asked him why he wanted to know.

'I ask you,' Hilder replied, 'because you said he was in bed here. He was not in bed here, was he?'

'It does not make any odds to you,' she answered him.

Then Hilder said, 'Ben was not a-bed here.' He was quite firm in his mind about that.

'Yes, he was,' she told him, 'by the side of me.'

Imagine her anger at the impudence of these probings. What had it to do with him who was where that night? And anyway, had he no sympathy for a woman only hours bereaved?

'Well, but Daniel was not,' Hilder said, persisting with his enquiry, knowing that both men were out of the house on their barn-breaking expedition.

'No, not beside me, but he was a-bed here.'

'But he wasn't,' Hilder insisted. And then he dropped his bombshell. 'I know that Daniel was not a-bed here for I know a man that saw Daniel. And William Russell, before him.'

Hannah was furious. 'I know well it was who told you that. It was Hawkins, damn him. He may as well keep his mouth shut.'

Thomas Hawkins, whom William Russell and Daniel had hoped might remain silent about their early morning meeting, had been spreading the word in a village agog at the mysterious death. He had blabbed to Hilder and others about seeing the two men in the wood.

Hannah had brought the conversation to a halt. She would say no more.

Discord evidently ruled in The Wheel, at least as far as Hannah and Ben were concerned. This was an important element of the prosecution case, drawing a portrait of a foul-mouthed, immoral termagant. Ananias Hilder was questioned in court about an argument between Hannah and her husband early on the Sunday afternoon. Ben and Hilder had been talking about a sow that Ben wished to sell. Enraged, Hannah had intervened, saying the sow was hers and that she had bought it. 'It was language not fit to be repeated,' Hilder told the court. 'She said, "No, ****, if he sells that sow, I'll sell him and that **** soon."'

There were several witnesses who told of the threats they had heard Hannah use in relation to her husband. A labourer, Thomas Relf, was at The Wheel about a fortnight before Ben's death. Hannah told him that she had had an argument with Ben. She said to Relf, 'I'll be the death of him before the summer is out.' Relf recalled that Daniel was present and that he had told her to be quiet and she had replied, 'I'll be cursed if I don't.' And Thomas Luck, a huxter who was another regular at The Wheel, said that he had heard her say more than once, 'I wish he would drop dead and never come back any more.'

James French had much the same tale to tell. He had heard Hannah say a number of times, and as recently as the Saturday before her husband's death, that she would kill him in some way or other. Other times he heard her say that she would be the death of him. He was unsure if Ben heard all of the threats because he was deaf.

Yet another witness, Mark Blackford, recalled that on one occasion Hannah told him, after Ben had gone out, that she hoped he would never come home again alive. She hoped that somebody would kill him.

'Surely you don't mean that,' Blackford had said.

'Yes, I do,' Hannah had answered. 'There are people about that I like more than I do him.'

And he had seen them together, Blackford said, Daniel and Hannah. They were very fond of each other. He had seen her sitting on his lap.

Not that everyone interpreted Hannah's remarks in quite the same way. Ann Hicks, one of Ben's nieces, had been in the house on one occasion and because he was late returning home Hannah was very angry. She had said that she would cut his throat, break his head, poison him when he got back. But Ann had thought these were mere words, the empty threats of an angry woman.

Thomas Evans, the Burwash surgeon, told the court that he had attended Ben frequently before his death although not during the two months immediately before. On Wednesday 10 May he had examined the body in the presence of two other medical men. The stomach and the intestines were greatly inflamed. In the stomach, Evans said,

> we found a considerable quantity of gross white powder adhering to it. We took the stomach home and analysed the contents by various tests, by which we sublimed nearly a drachm of white arsenic. A drachm would be quite sufficient to cause death, indeed much more than sufficient. A few grains would, I believe, be sufficient and a drachm contains 60 grains. I have no doubt that more than one drachm was taken by the deceased.

Robert Crowhurst, who had a shop at Burwash, testified to having sold arsenic to Hannah at the beginning of the month. Both Isaac and Joseph Oliver remembered being at The Wheel about three weeks before Ben died and seeing her put arsenic powder on a slice of bread which she said was for mice. They both said that she made no secret of spreading the powder on the bread and butter.

Then it was the turn of Isaac Oliver of Heathfield in the witness box, and he blew apart the smuggling tale. When he met Daniel on 10 May, he asked him if he had had anything to do with Ben's death. The suggestion was denied but Oliver was not convinced. 'I told him I would not believe but what he did,' he said. Daniel had admitted that they had been out barn-breaking and he told him where he and William Russell had hidden the wheat sacks. The following day Oliver had picked them up.

The prosecution case was undeniably strong. There had been a procession of credible witnesses who told tales of threats and who proffered accounts of an illicit affair. Then there was the evidence of the contradictory timings, intended, so the jury must have believed, to lead astray any who tried to work out when the poison had been administered. And Hannah had purchased a poison which was so easy to administer.

For the defence only one witness appeared. Richard Sinton, described as a little boy, said that he had spoken to Ben on the Sunday afternoon. He had complained of a pain in his chest and had told the boy that he did not expect to be alive on Monday. Neither of the accused had anything to say in their defence. But, so the *Hampshire Telegraph* tells us, 'the prisoners both maintained that callous hardihood which characterised their conduct during the whole trial'.

After a brief withdrawal the jury returned with a guilty verdict. Although the evidence had been purely circumstantial, it had been strong enough to persuade the jury of the couple's guilt. Hannah, asked if she had anything to say before sentence was pronounced, denied having committed murder, denouncing the evidence as false, part of the Russell family's vendetta against her. Daniel Leany, possibly overcome by circumstances, said nothing.

The two were sentenced to be hanged at Horsham on 31 July. Hannah was to be drawn to the place of execution on a hurdle, a remnant of the degrading punishment reserved for women who had done away with their husbands. Both were to be 'dissected and anatomised pursuant to the Statute in the case made and provided'. The *Hampshire Telegraph* comments with apparent satisfaction that 'the unhappy criminals are victims of impure affections – the woman being guilty of petty treason in having wilfully destroyed her husband by poison and the man, her unlawful paramour, with having aided and abetted her in the crime'.

At the time, in accordance with the law, all convicted of murder were to be fed on bread and water and hanged within two days. After this conviction, however, the judge appeared to have some doubt about the correctness of the verdict as far as Hannah was concerned. She had been charged as a principal, whereas from the evidence it did not appear that she was 'present, aiding and abetting the alleged murder'. As a result she was respited to give time for a more sober consideration of the matter.

For Daniel Leany, too, there was a respite 'for the humane purpose of further investigating his guilt'. But no extenuating circumstances were discovered, and he was executed on Thursday 2 August. Afterwards his body was taken to the surgeon for dissection.

In the days leading up his execution Daniel admitted to smuggling and poaching, but not to murder. The *Sussex Advertiser* reports sadly: 'This declaration, although repeatedly cautioned as to the awful consequences of denying the truth, he persisted in to the last moment.' His last morning he spent time in prayer with the chaplain and took communion. At noon he was led from his cell to the platform in front of the gaol. 'His expression of countenance was mild and placid and he looked to be a mere boy.' And of course, he was a mere boy. He spoke to Mr Weston of Burwash who was with him before the execution and said some things about Burwash people connected with him in his illegal pursuits 'who have hitherto escaped suspicion'. And then the white hood was put on his head.

As far as Hannah Russell was concerned, her respite was prolonged by the need to ensure that the correct legal procedures had been followed. This allowed time for what today would be called campaigners to argue her case. What now came under scrutiny was the medical evidence. Had Ben Russell really died of arsenic poisoning?

Dr Gideon Mantell, the celebrated palaeontologist who lived in Lewes, had followed the case very closely, especially its medico-legal aspects, and in the courtroom on the day of the trial he became increasingly concerned about Dr Evans's evidence. He was concerned that Dr Evans's procedures had not been strictly scientific. Mantell scribbled a note to defence counsel, Mr Platt, who had had only two hours to prepare his defence, suggesting specific questions for cross-examination. But then Mantell was called away suddenly to attend to a patient. When he returned to the court the verdict had been reached and the sentence handed down.

Mantell was unable to do anything about Daniel Leany, but he devoted considerable time to Hannah's case. He forwarded his reservations about the medical evidence to the High Sheriff, who immediately laid it before the judge. Impressed, Mr Baron

Graham encouraged Mantell to investigate the case as fully as possible. Assisted by Mr Ellis, the solicitor for the defence, and Mr Weston of Burwash, who had never believed the pair guilty, Mantell obtained enough fresh material to persuade the judge that there were grounds for doubting that Ben Russell had been poisoned. Why, for example, had there been no reports of excessive vomiting, of debilitating diarrhoea, of excruciating stomach pains?

On 5 October 1826 Mantell records in his diary: 'Have been much engaged in attempting to investigate the case of a poor woman now under sentence of death at Horsham, having been convicted of poisoning her husband. Circumstances occurred which led me to believe that the surgeon's evidence was founded on incorrect experiments. Went twice to Burwash to learn particulars of the affair.'

Dr Gideon Algernon Mantell.

In the following months Mantell, still the tireless questing scientist, still the conscientious local doctor, busied himself seeking other medical and scientific advice. He paid regular visits to Burwash to speak to local people, especially those who had been witnesses at the trial. Ignorance and deep prejudice were difficult to overcome, and he encountered great resistance to his enquiries. Through the autumn and winter of 1826 Mantell struggled to collect his evidence but eventually he produced a report which he sent to Robert Peel, the Home Secretary. Its main points cast doubt on Dr Evans's claim that Ben Russell died of arsenic poisoning; it even questioned the statement that his stomach contained arsenic and dismissed as unsatisfactory the tests for arsenic which Evans had carried out.

According to Mantell, even if there was a drachm of arsenic in the stomach, Russell would not have died so suddenly. At about half-past nine Russell, hale and hearty, had talked to his father. And yet within four hours he was dead. Eminent medical men opined that no dose of arsenic could have occasioned death in so short a period. The shortest time recorded was four hours in the case of a woman who committed suicide by swallowing a quarter of a pound of the poison. And Mantell quoted two cases in his own practice at Lewes. In one, a delicate woman took nearly two ounces of arsenic and did not die for six hours. In the second case, a boy took a large spoonful of arsenic mixed with treacle. He walked 200 yards and then fell down in agony, was carried home – but it took 24 hours for him to die. Mantell's conclusion was that Russell, who for some time had had heart trouble, had died of angina following the physical exertion of carrying the sack of wheat.

On 26 February 1827 Mantell was able to write in his diary: 'Yesterday morning received the gratifying intelligence that Hannah Russell, the poor woman who was in Horsham jail under sentence of death, was pardoned and set at liberty, in consequence of my communication to the Secretary of State, Mr Peel. Made some observations on the case before the Mechanics Institute.'

Now, declared innocent of her husband's murder, Hannah was regarded rather differently by *The Times*: 'It is gratifying to state that the conduct of Hannah Russell during the whole time of her confinement in Horsham jail has been most exemplary.' It added an appeal to her former neighbours to view her past suffering with regret and 'to receive her among them in the spirit of Christian charity and benevolence'. As for Daniel's execution, 'It would now appear that he was guiltless of the crime for which he paid the penalty of death.'

But if the wider world was now convinced of the innocence of Hannah and Daniel, that smaller isolated corner of Burwash was less so. She returned to the village, though not to The Wheel. Regardless of the law, regardless of justice, the Vestry members had not changed their minds about her. Widowed and with her child Mary, she went to live with a shoemaker, Thomas Chandler. On 15 June 1827, with Frank Russell in the chair, the Vestry 'resolved that Thomas Chandler be not employed by the Parish whilst Hannah Russell is living with him'. Previously Chandler had had a contract to make shoes for the parish poor.

On 19 May 1830 Mantell writes:

On to Burwash by 1 o'clock. Dined; saw Hannah Russell, the poor woman whose life we had saved some years since. She is married [to Thomas Chandler] and has conducted herself irreproachably. Much interested in her artless and affecting account of her feelings while under sentence of death; a consciousness of her innocence deprived her situation of all its bitterness: she said she 'was as happy as the day is long.' Where ignorance is bliss 'tis folly to be wise! A cultivated mind would have felt the most agonising suspense under such circumstances. Of her innocence there can be no doubt; yet for this supposed crime a poor lad of 19 was executed. The Jury consisted of inhabitants of Burwash; men already prejudiced against the poor creatures.

Hannah was still living in the village in March 1869 when the Rector, John Coker Egerton, wrote admiringly of her in his diary: 'Hannah Chandler, a wonderfully tough old woman & hangs onto life very tightly.' Only a few years earlier, Egerton had referred to Frank Russell, now well into his eighties, as 'an old smuggler but he has amassed a good deal of Money'.

But all there was left of Daniel Leany were tales of a ghost in Gladish Wood, 'a ragged thing that clutches its throat as it blunders through the undergrowth, creating terror in those whom he may encounter'.

Was the prosecution case as strong as it appeared all those years ago in the courtroom at Lewes? There were all the threats that witnesses had heard but perhaps they were as harmless as Ben's niece, Ann Hicks, said they were. Just the angry words of an exasperated wife.

And really it is difficult to get much mileage out of the purchase of arsenic. Arsenic was the cure for mice, and people all over the country, long before the 'Little Nipper' was invented, went to the local shop to purchase it in small quantities. But there were those who in the weeks before her husband's death had actually seen Hannah spread it on a slice of bread. What about that, then? But mouse poison had to be put on something. On a morsel of cheese, on a few grains of sugar, so why not on bread? It was done in other households. So it is difficult to prove murderous intent or murder in fact simply on the strength of buying arsenic.

It did not help the accused when they were found to have told conflicting tales in the days succeeding the discovery of the body. And yet William Russell, in his anxiety to save the family name, was responsible for that. Supposing that, after hiding the wheat sacks, he and Daniel had carried the body back to The Wheel and had given out that Ben had died in the night at home. What then? There might, of course, have been a similar enquiry, they might well have been charged in exactly the same way, but at least the two accused would not have been presented from the start as confirmed liars with something to hide.

A rural *cause célèbre*, then, there's no doubt about that. An appalling miscarriage of justice? Mantell and others thought so.

And yet . . . It's a minor matter, perhaps something scarcely worth referring to. Remember when Robert Bowles called in at The Wheel on the Monday morning. He had not then heard about Ben's death and Hannah made no mention of it though she already knew that her husband was dead. In conversation she did say something quite odd. She said that sometime earlier that morning she had been alarmed by a noise upstairs. She had come to believe that it was an omen of death, either of her husband or of a relative. Now that bang, or whatever it was supposed to be, was often talked about in times more superstitious than today. An unexplained noise was a presage of death. But it is difficult now not to believe that Hannah was trying to suggest that some supernatural effect, some non-human agency, had announced her husband's death. There she was, in that gloomy old bar, in a quite casual way referring to a death that she already knew had taken place.

That kind of red herring, if that is what it was, may incline the sceptical to believe that Hannah was a cunning, callous woman, composed enough to chatter away to one of her early customers, knowing all the time that her newly dead husband now lay abandoned in Gladish Wood. There is something that jars here, makes one a shade uncertain of her. Is she too cool, too prepared, already too much at ease?

So was Ben Russell poisoned by his unfaithful wife? Was Daniel Leany unlucky to come up against a jury prejudiced against a young adulterer? Was Thomas Evans wrong in his medical assessment, as Mantell said he was?

These questions were asked in 1826. They have never since been satisfactorily answered.

4

THE DISMEMBERMENT IN DONKEY ROW

Brighton, 1831

Look at him. This is John Holloway. What sort of man does he seem? Has he the face of a Bible-spouting true believer? Can you see him as a boy delivering religious pamphlets? Does he look like a one-time Sunday school teacher? Because that is what he was.

Is this a young fellow – young because he will never be old – just gone to the bad, a petty thief, capable of stealing a watch and chain from a drunken man? Does he look the type to persuade a servant-girl to let him guard her trunk and then, when her back is turned, to steal the quarter's wages she has inside? Can you see such duplicity in his features?

He has led a rough, dangerous life at sea and on land. Is he courageous looking?

And the ladies' man, any sign of that? We know about Sarah Johnson, whom he truly loved – or so he said; we know about Sarah Harman too. Then there was Celia Bashford, whom he married, and Maria Burke, whom he did not. There was Sarah Sanders, whose end is such a puzzle. And Ann Kennett, who was with him that awful night in Donkey Row. There was another woman he set up in her own house. He left her before the rent fell due. And there were prostitutes. And others more innocent, for he was a practised seducer. A ladies' man, yes, even if he had little love for most of them and not a hint of constancy for any. Are you surprised to learn he was a bigamist?

John Holloway, painted in Horsham Gaol by J. Perez at the request of his mother, 1831.

But the real question must be: is this the face of a murderer? Can you discern in his features that cold, murderous quality which he surely had? Or does it not show in this portrait? Not even the aching fear he must have experienced when it was painted, for he knew then, as he sat in Horsham Gaol, that in weeks he must surely hang?

Other things are similarly concealed. You cannot tell that he is barely five feet tall. Nor that, even if he cannot spell well, he writes fluently, convincingly, with style and confidence. In gaol awaiting trial he writes extensively about his past in 'The Atrocious murder of Celia Holloway'. For a man who has wasted much of his short life, he writes very impressively. Other evidence will suggest that he is a fluent speaker too. He can persuade people. Especially women.

First, though, consider him when very young.

John William Holloway, born in Lewes in May 1806, was taken almost straight away to live with his grandparents at Litlington, for his father was away at the wars and his mother, as an army wife, shared her husband's campaigns. Some time later, with his father now discharged, they all, grandparents, parents and children, lived in Litlington. Later, he went to Alfriston National School where, aged ten, eleven or so, he was appointed pupil–teacher. In those days young Holloway attended the very active chapel in Alfriston and years later the minister would recall his good qualities.

At some stage, in about 1818 perhaps, the family moved to Brighton, a growing town, a vibrant place, of 45,000 inhabitants, where an old soldier's family might have better opportunities.

In the early years at Brighton the chapel played a significant part in the youngster's life. Every waking hour on a Sunday, if we are to believe his account, was devoted to prayer, to scripture reading, to chapel going. And time on weekdays, too, was found for these activities.

So then, what happened?

Holloway claimed that he fell in with bad company; that he started to drink, to leave off regular chapel attendance, to become an unreliable worker. Nevertheless, this descent into idleness, unreliability and then petty dishonesties is sudden. It is so out of character. Have we missed something? Was it always there in him, a crude quality, a vicious, callous streak? Did the dangerous man always lurk there?

At Brighton Races, Holloway, then seventeen, met a 28-year-old servant-girl, Celia Bashford. How she loved him! he said.

'She was never happy but when with me; but as I did not love her, I only laughed at her folly; and, to tell the truth, I was ashamed to be seen with her until after dark and then to get out of the town and on the hills as soon as possible.'

Perhaps the age disparity was an embarrassment. Or was it her appearance? Her disproportionately large head? Her diminutive stature, for she was only four foot three? Her long arms, the hands turned outwards 'like the paws of a mole'?

Over the next year or two he went out with her, although he left Brighton for some months to try to find a ship, but failed. On the way home, he did some begging; he stole a watch and chain from a sleeping drunk.

Then he returned to Brighton and it is possible that he left and came back on other occasions. He was no longer settled. But he met Sarah Johnson. His friends, he claimed, persuaded him to give her up. Why they did so he never explained. Would there not have been greater pressure, even if unspoken, for him to finish with Celia? Sarah Harman was another girl he spent time with, but that didn't last either. He gave her up. Or so he says. Might it not be possible that these young women gave him up? Had they even then seen something in his nature which made them uneasy?

And then Celia, a thirty-year-old woman now, revealed that she was pregnant. Holloway, only nineteen, resisted marriage and found himself clapped in Lewes Gaol by the Overseers of Ardingly, Celia's home parish. Would he guarantee to support her? They wanted no further responsibility for bastards. He could look after her and the prospective infant or he could stay where he was.

After five weeks Holloway relented, was released, went to Ardingly and married. Then the parish officers told him they would not let him stay there. Had he work? No? Well then, he could take himself and his wife to his own parish. Let them have the keeping of them. Why should Ardingly be lumbered with an out-of-work husband and his wife and child?

Resentful, Holloway and Celia returned to Brighton. After some days in the workhouse in separate wings, they moved into lodgings in the town, with furniture bought by Holloway's father.

He had learnt now, he said, that Celia had not been made pregnant by him but by someone called Edward Goldsmith. She always denied this and perhaps this is just one of several instances of Holloway seeking to justify his own unfaithfulness. The child was stillborn and Holloway would brood on his ill-fortune and on his marriage to a woman he would come to call 'a repellent object'.

Holloway next found work with a bookseller, William Nute, a Wesleyan who was never to desert Holloway, who stayed with him even to his last moments. Nute would always testify to the young man's good work. Good or no, however, Holloway gave up the job, though whether he had other work to go to is uncertain. It seems unlikely, for the couple were soon in desperate need.

When Maria Burke, a fifteen-year-old, came to share their lodgings, matters came to 'a very improper pass'. But then things always would, for Holloway had a taste for the ladies. And even if Maria at least eased the problems with the rent, the Holloways continued to be hard up.

In desperation, Celia wrote to her brother for money. Half-way between Henfield and Brighton, Holloway met his brother-in-law, who gave him fifteen shillings to tide them over. And it would have done had not Holloway spent most of it at a pub on the way home.

Celia's brother was at the house within days. There was a fearful row. It ended with Celia going home to Ardingly, taking the furniture with her, for which the brother gave Holloway two sovereigns. He was to brood on that too. After all, his father had given them the furniture. How he resented Celia's family!

With Celia gone, there was an interlude with Maria Burke, who stayed on in the bare rooms until Holloway was persuaded by his parents to give her up. These relationships with women were often frail. Just as he had been persuaded to give up Sarah Johnson, so with Maria Burke.

Then, free of domestic encumbrances, Holloway went to sea, signing on for one trip on a collier, but he did not re-sign, claiming that the ship's master was against him. When he tried to enlist on a man-of-war, he was ordered off the ship by the captain, who considered him unsuitable. What was it that prevented Holloway from being taken on in a fleet which accommodated both the best and worst of men?

Then it was back to Brighton to work as a builder, but he was accused of some dishonesty or other – again there are no details – and he either left or was dismissed.

After this, Celia returned to Brighton and Holloway took up with her once more, but it was not successful. There were arguments; he was drunk at times; he manhandled her; there were other women. He had never loved Celia: he was coming to hate her.

Yet Celia does not seem to have been so hateful a woman. The evidence certainly speaks in her favour. One of her former employers, a woman with whom she was in service, wrote: 'I was very sorry when she married John Holloway as I was afraid he would not use her well; and it is well known that he frequently left her and took up with others. She would frequently say to me she would not mind dying under his hands for she always thought she should.'

And there were other testimonies to her good character from her landlord and his wife and her own sister.

In September 1827, with Celia again pregnant, Holloway, still only twenty-one, left home once more, this time to join the Blockade Service. He was in the Service for four years until its disbandment. He served at sea and in watch-towers on shore. It was hard, demanding work and naval discipline was severe. Yet Holloway seems not to have complained. Rather, the impression is given when he writes of this period that for him it was an enjoyable time. He makes no mention of encounters with smugglers either at sea or on land, but it is inconceivable that he was not involved in the highly dangerous struggles at times.

For a period he was based at Rye, and here he met Sarah Sanders.

'I acknowledge that I did promise to marry her soon after our acquaintance began,' Holloway confesses. He had joined the Service under the name of Goldsmith, his mother's surname and incidentally the surname of the man whom he had accused of Celia's first pregnancy. Certainly his adoption of this name would have made for fewer complications had he committed bigamy with Sarah Sanders. But it was not to be. He discovered that 'she was a girl of very bad character'.

She was inconstant. She had another lover. Such infidelity on the part of a woman – on the part of his woman – was insupportable.

'We quarrelled and I was heard to threaten her by a woman of the name of Frost. From that time to the present I have never, to my knowledge, seen her.'

And then he continues:

But it happened, after I was gone from Rye, that a young woman was found dead, apparently washed on shore; and I think it was said when found that she had a rope around her neck; but the particulars I do not know as I was not there at the time. I only know what I heard when I returned; and I believe it was likewise said that she was in the family way, and her earrings torn out of her ears; and in many other respects her body had the marks of violence on it.

Now after this young woman was found [Holloway goes on], it was observed that Sarah Sanders was missing and that the last time she was seen was in my company and that she was likewise in the family way. It was immediately said that the young woman that was found was the said Sarah Sanders. On hearing of this, Mrs Frost went forward and stated that she heard me threaten her very much and that she believed the deceased was the said Sarah Sanders and that she had not been seen since. On this evidence a warrant issued out for my apprehension.

Holloway was questioned on the matter but his captain is alleged to have given him an alibi. He said that Holloway was away at sea when the girl was alleged to have been murdered. Just a few years later, however, doubts were to be expressed about the thoroughness of the investigation into this case.

So was it sheer bad luck that Holloway should have been implicated in this murder? Was the girl washed up on shore the one that he had threatened? Or was Sarah Sanders alive and well and now away from the district?

'God is my witness,' says Holloway. 'I am innocent of that murder.'

And at this distance in time, we must allow him his innocence.

Then also at Rye he met Ann Kennett, a dressmaker. She was then about twenty years old and had two illegitimate children. What developed was a real love affair, Holloway tells us. When he came off watch, at whatever hour, he would walk the five miles to Rye to see Ann, presumably to sleep with her and then return to duty at the watch house.

How are we to view Ann Kennett?

Are we to see her as 'very sociable and comfortable . . . a harmless and inoffensive woman . . . a good sort of woman'? She was described by different witnesses in these terms.

Or just the opposite? 'The Atrocious Murder' contains Holloway's confessions and an account of his life, but these are wrapped within a commentary. Ann Kennett is described by the commentator as 'one of the most finished fiends which the history of the female sex can produce'.

A significant event which can be dated in the uncertain chronology of Holloway's career is recorded in the Rye Parish Records. (Ann had become pregnant again.) 'William Goldsmith of the parish of Winchelsea, bachelor, and Ann Kennett of this parish, spinster, were married by licence, in the parish church of Rye, the 16th day of March, 1830, by J.S. Myers, officiating minister.'

Goldsmith. Bachelor. Holloway. Bigamist.

As for Celia, he admitted that 'he did not care what became of her'. Their one-year-old daughter, Agnes, their second child, had died; Celia was destitute, living on the parish, earning a few pence selling pins and cotton from a tray. It was not any concern of his.

Early the following year, Holloway was discharged from the Blockade Service. He and Ann Kennett – she had miscarried – went to Brighton seeking work. Almost straight away Celia knew of their arrival but she was not concerned to have her

Page 162.

The record of Holloway's bigamous marriage at Rye. He signs himself as Wm Goldsmith; she makes her mark. (Courtesy of East Sussex Record Office: Rye Parish Record Office ESRO PAR 467/1/31)

husband back. Although she knew he and Ann were living together under the name of Goldsmith, she was not aware of their bigamous marriage. This was of little importance to Celia. She had become accustomed to being without him. But she did need money.

Fearing that Celia would have the Parish Overseers chasing him for cash, Holloway left the town, taking Ann Kennett with him. In his account of this period, Holloway says that he now became a coiner, a forger, boasting of being able to pass sovereigns and shillings and of being generally successful at it. He bought a cloak and was accepted – in some circles – as a gentleman. He and Ann worked their way along the coast, spending time at Eastbourne and Hastings and enjoying some extravagant living. Returning to Brighton, Holloway recounts how he picked up a woman and put her in comfortable lodgings with a servant. He passed her off as his wife and promised to marry her. Then, just as suddenly, he left her.

It was no joke, he writes. It was the woman's own fault. Women should look out for themselves; they should not allow themselves to be taken in. Men will always make fools of women if they can.

Then the coining stopped; the money ran short; he was desperate for work. There is no explanation for this change in his fortunes. Perhaps Holloway had exaggerated his success.

In the late spring of 1831, the couple found lodgings at 7 Margaret Street. It was a poor terraced house, the best he could afford from the wages of his new employment as a painter working on the Royal Chain Pier. The house was conveniently situated for his work. Only months earlier he had quit Brighton because of Celia. Now he was back, living only a short walk from her lodgings, which were at 4 Cavendish Place.

As might be expected, as soon as she learnt of his presence, in early May she applied to the Overseers of the Poor. She wanted maintenance to ease her desperate poverty.

No. 7 Margaret Street, where Holloway and Kennett planned the murder. (Alan Skinner)

Though he cannot have been surprised, he was reluctant to pay – and angry too. Why should he pay for a woman he did not love, a woman he had been tricked into marrying, a woman who with her family had always caused him difficulties?

It is not possible to say when Ann Kennett learnt of her true status or of her so-called husband's real name. Perhaps she knew of the circumstances before leaving Rye. Whatever the truth of the matter, she must have known the answer to these questions by mid-June when Holloway and Celia met the parish officers. He agreed to pay 2s per week maintenance.

Then heavy rain over several days caused Holloway to be laid off work. Within three weeks he could afford to send her only 1s 6d and later he could manage only a shilling.

He and Celia argued over this.

Ann Kennett was usually the bearer of the money. She was later to say that on occasion she pawned clothing to make up the deficit. Holloway related how she was always kind to Celia, taking her butter, tea, eggs, bacon. But then, why not take her the few pence she was owed if they could afford the food?

Amelia Simmonds, at whose house Celia lodged, explained in court how Ann Kennett had brought a shilling on 4 July.

'Is that all you have brought me?' Celia asked her. 'I have nothing to eat. What am I to do with a shilling? I will go to the Overseer to know which John is to keep – his wife or his whore.' She took the poker and struck Kennett twice. Kennett took hold of her and said, 'You are too little to hit, but mind, you shall suffer for this.'

Holloway went round to 4 Cavendish Place that evening. Why, he asked Celia, had she gone to the Overseer again? 'Madam,' he said, 'you think you are going to frighten me but you are mistaken.'

And as he left he shouted, 'You damned bitch, you shall suffer for this before many days.'

A witness was warned by Holloway not to interfere. 'You don't know as much about me as a great many or you would mind your p's and q's.'

Celia does, however, present us with another unsolved mystery. She was heavily pregnant again. Was it another man or was it Holloway? Had Celia slept with him? Whatever the truth, could Celia, deformed, unloved by her husband, impoverished, be blamed if she had sought comfort or affection from some other man?

The argument on 4 July marked the date when Holloway resolved to rid himself of Celia. He began by forbidding her to visit his mother, and she seems to have obeyed him in this, not visiting the old woman in the last days of her life. As a consequence, when she went missing, Mrs Holloway assumed that she had left Brighton for London, which was the tale that Holloway put about.

But if he was to kill her, he needed her away from Cavendish Place. And this is where his plan becomes cumbersome. He planned that Celia should die in another house and sought a suitable place to rent. Eventually he found one in North Steine Row – better known as Donkey Row. It was a short distance across the road from The Pavilion. And remarkably it was only a hundred yards or so from Cavendish Place.

Incredibly, Celia fell in with her husband's scheme. Only ten days earlier, they had been at loggerheads: by Thursday, 14 July, she was quite prepared to go with him to start a new life together.

Where? He did not tell her. But she thought it was London somewhere.

Perhaps he intended it to be a surprise; perhaps that is how he passed it off. Holloway must have been at his most persuasive. His treatment of Celia over the years had been monstrous. Only days before, it had been plain that he not only loved Ann but that he hated Celia. Yet, within the space of days, he had persuaded her to go with him, her violent, unreliable husband, to an unknown destination. Did Celia not pause to reflect?

And what about Ann Kennett? Had he suggested that he intended to give her up? Did none of Celia's friends or relatives express their doubts? How could any one of them have brought themselves to believe what they were hearing? Should a woman, due to have a child within two weeks, be troubled in this way, at this time? Did no one wonder about that? Were they all equally persuaded by Holloway? Did he really reassure them that they were off to London for a new start?

On 14 July, Holloway called at Cavendish Place. He had come for Celia's clothes. He would also take the bed and mattress. He had found some temporary lodgings, he said. They were going into them before leaving for London.

Holloway told her that he would come back for her later in the day. She gave him a penny for a half-pint of beer and went off to the bakery to buy him a bread pudding for his dinner.

Holloway went off with the trunk, the bed and the mattress to Donkey Row. Perhaps he had already borrowed the wheelbarrow that he needed for later. Ann Kennett was waiting in the house.

We are asked to believe that this was the first time Holloway revealed his intentions to Ann. But for what reason had she gone to Donkey Row? They already had lodgings. Now, Holloway, laden down with Celia's property, explained to Ann Kennett what he planned. But what was her response? She loved Holloway; she recognised Celia as an obstacle as well as a constant drain on their uncertain finances. But murder is another matter. Even if they had earlier spoken in a wishful sort of way of Celia's death; even if they had hypothesised about it, this was reality. We are expected to believe that, one mid-morning, Holloway informed Ann Kennett that he intended to murder his wife in a few hours' time. Is it believable? It is believable only if Ann Kennett is the fiend that the commentator in Holloway's 'Atrocious Murder' believed her to be.

But suppose her innocent. What then were her possible courses of action? She could have warned Celia; she could have told the parish constable; she could have begged friends to intercede, to persuade Holloway of the madness of his plan. Or she might simply have left him. She must have realised where his violent nature was leading them.

Yet all she did was to try to make him change his mind because she feared he might be caught.

Holloway later confessed to frightening her into compliance but even so it is difficult to believe.

Here is Holloway: 'She said I had better not do it for fear of being discovered. I told her I would trust to that if she would assist me; she said, yes, she would.'

It does not seem to have been much of a struggle.

Holloway continues: 'As I had got the clothes, we knew not hardly how to dispose of them.'

This is interesting. It proves that the clothes were not taken simply to make money. They had been got out of the house so that it would appear that Celia had planned to go to London. Had she disappeared, with the clothes still at Cavendish Place, suspicions would have been instantly aroused.

Ann Kennett stayed in 11 Donkey Row while Holloway went back to Cavendish Place. Did she have any doubts as she sat in the empty house, bare of furniture, with only Celia's trunk, bed and mattress? Did she dread Holloway's return? She knew what was to be done when he came.

Did Holloway himself, with Celia in tow, entertain any doubts? It does not seem so.

When Holloway and Celia reached the southern end of Donkey Row, he told her to wait while he went into the house. He had made some excuse, of course. A friend of his was sharing the house, he said, and he might be asleep. Holloway did not wish to waken him. He would first check, go to the house, see what the man was doing.

So Celia waited in the late afternoon sun, looking up the street at the blank-walled terraced houses, at number 11, the only house with shutters.

In the house, Holloway instructed Ann Kennett to wait in the cupboard in the corner of the room.

'I then went and called Celia. When she was in the house I shut the door, told her I wanted to wait a little while because my partner lived upstairs and he was in bed and we must wait until he got up and with that pretence I kept her in conversation for some time.'

They went across the brick-floored downstairs room to the open stairway.

'I asked her to sit down on the stairs and then on the pretence of kissing her I passed a line around her neck and strangled her.'

So the pregnant, despised, much-abused Celia, only moments before she died, must have come to believe that her husband was at last turning over a new leaf. Poor Celia, deceived to the very end.

And then, surely, a stroke of genius. Murderer's genius, that is.

For just suppose that, at some future time, they were no longer lovers, Ann and he. Suppose that for some or other reason she decided to tell what had happened at Donkey Row. There can be no other reason for what occurred next than that Holloway determined to involve Ann Kennett yet more deeply in the crime.

'As soon as I passed the line around her neck, I found it was rather more than I could manage,' he says.

Nonsense. Holloway was a strong enough man, strong enough to murder tiny Celia, the pregnant woman with the mole-like hands.

'I called Ann and God knows she assisted me by taking hold of each end of the rope with me and she held the rope with me till the poor girl dropped.'

And these words implicate Ann Kennett, make her equally guilty with her lover.

Holloway continues, giving Ann some Lady Macbeth-like lines.

'I held the cord for a time myself and Ann made use of this expression, "Do not let your heart fail you".'

Did Ann Kennett encourage him thus? She was supposed to have been presented with the murder plan only hours before. Were those witnesses who spoke highly of her totally wrong? Or was Holloway the only liar and monster?

'When I thought she was dead, or nearly dead,' Holloway goes on, 'I dragged her into a cupboard or coal hole under the stairs and under the stairs there is some nails. I did not remove the cord but took an over-handed knot and I made the ends fast to the nails so that she was hanging by the neck.'

It was all the work of minutes. Celia had come away from Cavendish Place not half an hour earlier. She must have been in 11 Donkey Row no more than five minutes before she was strung up in the cupboard.

And next? Well, she could not be left there.

'I proposed then cutting her. Ann Kennett told me to wait until the blood settled.'

So the body was left and they started a fire in the grate, burning some of those items of clothing, bonnets and the like, which were unlikely to be pawned. But while this went on, they knew that other work awaited them.

On the following morning, they returned to Donkey Row. There was the mattress they had brought and Holloway poured the chaff filling out of it. He needed the ticken, the mattress cover.

Then he set to.

I cut off the head first and I think the arms I carried with the head. Ann Kennett was present. I never went to the house to do anything with the body but what I took Ann Kennett with me. And the day that I brought the head and the other parts away, she was to walk behind me to see if any blood came through. The first attempt we made would not do because the blood came through the ticken. Ann told me of it and we went back and put it into a little box and then into the ticken.

The head and limbs which Holloway severed on the brick floor of the downstairs room were taken back to Margaret Street. Ann had previously asked one of her neighbours not to lock the back door, explaining that Holloway would be out late, smuggling. When that night they returned, together with the box with its awful contents in the mattress cover, they let themselves into the back area. They dropped the contents of the box into the common privy.

The rest of Celia Holloway was still at the house in Donkey Row. It had been placed in the trunk which had held Celia's clothes.

Ann had washed the floor. Washed it and washed it.

The next day she went to the pawnshop, pledging three gowns and an apron, giving her name as Ann Goldsmith. When she returned later with other articles she gave the name Brown and said that she lived in Carlton Row.

That night Holloway and Ann returned to Donkey Row. They carried out the trunk, placing it on the wheelbarrow. He led the way pushing the barrow, she following with a pick and shovel.

Along the London Road they went with their appalling cargo, past the Hare & Hounds, silent and dark, and on beyond the bounds of the town. Well into the country now, nearing Preston village, yet still only a couple of miles from Donkey Row. Here they turned up the footpath leading to a copse near Lovers' Walk.

Holloway, with Ann Kennett following, passes the Hare & Hounds on the way to Lovers' Walk.

The copse in Lovers' Walk where Celia Holloway's body was found.

Though Holloway was to recall it as a beautiful night, it was too dark to dig a grave. They put the trunk, the pick and shovel under some bushes, returning home with the barrow. As soon as it was light the following morning they were back at the intended burial place. It was difficult to dig much of a hole because of the tangle of tree roots. In the end, confessing himself defeated, Holloway stopped digging. The torso was flung out of the box and into the shallow hole and immediately covered with soil. Then the wooden trunk was broken up and the pieces scattered about. That evening Holloway and his mistress returned to retrieve the pick and shovel which they had left hidden under the bushes.

Some days later Holloway went back to the site to check the grave. On two other occasions, Ann Kennett visited. There seemed to be no cause for worry.

Yet they must have been anxious. People in Donkey Row had seen them coming and going. Those living there must have asked themselves why there had been so much activity for two or three days and why this had suddenly stopped.

Others too must have raised questions. Those in Cavendish Place and Margaret Street must certainly have been puzzled. But when questions were raised with Holloway, he informed them that Celia had found work as a chambermaid in London. She had taken all her clothes with her, he told people.

Did Holloway and Ann Kennett feel safe?

The guilty couple moved away from Margaret Street at the end of the week following the murder. But they went only as far as lodgings in neighbouring High Street. In the end, they were among the same people, walking the same streets. And the whole tacky business, the unsatisfactory story with all its loose ends about Celia's move, must have haunted them.

And how did Ann Kennett feel when one evening she met her lover with a prostitute on his arm? When she remonstrated with him, he hit her, cutting her forehead. This was only weeks after that fearful event which one might have thought had bound them for life.

It was the heavy rain only a week or so after the hasty burial that shifted the earth. Just the smallest piece of red cotton appeared on the surface. And when labourer Daniel Mascall passed that way on 25 July he wondered about it and the newly turned earth. When he pulled at the cotton a length of cloth appeared. And he wondered again.

Days later Mascall and a friend, Abraham Gillom, went together and considered the soil. When they poked it with a stick it smelt strong and unpleasant. But they never said a word to anybody in authority. It was not until 13 August that Gillom, his mother, sister and friend made an expedition to inspect the plot that Mascall had first seen three weeks earlier. After consideration, they decided to call in the parish constable. He brought a spade with him. There was a bundle of clothing tied with string and inside the headless, limbless torso with a male foetus protruding from it.

In the course of the day the news spread as Celia's remains were removed to a nearby barn. Thousands were attracted to the site, some of whom, for payment, were allowed sight of the body. Others searched the fields and hedgerows for the missing head and limbs or any other exciting souvenirs.

By evening, it was news in Brighton that a body had been found. Old Mrs Holloway heard about it. She had already had a dream that something dreadful had happened to Celia. Now she sought out her son. He, too, had heard what people were saying. But he was able to reassure his mother. Celia had gone to London. He had seen her off as far as Preston. She intended to catch the first coach to London. And he said that he had given her £9; she had saved £1 of her own money.

Late on the Saturday evening, on the very day that Gillom and the others had visited the site where Celia lay, the lovers, Holloway and Kennett, were placed under arrest.

The following evening, Sunday 14 August, an inquest was held at The Crown & Anchor in Preston. Outside, a huge crowd jostled, trying to catch a glimpse of the principals and the activities within. Had they been able to see, they might have noticed the bookcase which had been placed between Holloway and Ann Kennett to prevent their communicating. And had those outside been able to hear, they might have listened to Catherine Bishop, the dead woman's sister, relate the sad history of Celia's marriage; to Dr Hargreaves telling the coroner's jury that Celia had gone into labour at the time she was being done to death; to Amelia Simmonds identifying the pieces of wood as belonging to the trunk in which Celia's clothes had been removed.

At the end the jury returned a verdict of Wilful Murder against Holloway. He was sent to Horsham Gaol. Ann Kennett was remanded for further questioning and sent to Lewes House of Correction.

The crowd at the Crown & Anchor in Preston where the coroner's inquest was held. The painting is by J. Perez.

That same evening the common privy at Margaret Street was emptied. Near the bottom were found the stockinged legs, the arms still in their sleeves, and, inside the mattress cover, Celia's head.

Small wonder that *The Times* was to report on 16 August that 'the town of Brighton and for miles around has been thrown into the greatest excitation which was not exceeded by the horrible death of Maria Marten in the Red Barn at Polstead'.

There followed a number of examinations of Holloway at Horsham, and of Ann Kennett, first at the Sea House Inn in Brighton and later at Lewes.

For a time, Holloway stuck by his story that he had accompanied Celia to Preston, from where she intended to catch a coach to London.

Ann, meanwhile, was asked to explain the shattered trunk. Dissatisfied with what they heard, she was remanded by the magistrates for a further examination.

On Saturday 27 August Holloway asked to see the Brighton minister, Edward Everard. He was now anxious to take full responsibility for the crime. He wished to confess. In front of three magistrates, and unprompted by questions, he gave a fluent account of all that had occurred.

Holloway admitted that he had strangled his wife and cut up her body. He blamed her family for their unkindness to him. Because they had done all in their power to make him wretched, and because Celia herself had done her utmost to destroy his peace of mind, he had been driven to the act, for he had been determined on revenge.

This was a highly charged, emotional outpouring. 'His cries, yes, almost his shrieks for the mercy of God upon his soul, were most humble, most appalling,' the Revd Mr Everard said about this first confession.

Ann Kennett underwent another examination on Monday 29 August, when her neighbours from Margaret Street spoke of seeing her and Holloway carrying a parcel late at night. She was remanded for a further week. Eventually she was bound over to appear at the Winter Assizes.

Early in September, Holloway wrote several letters to his mother, acknowledging his guilt, assuring her of his repentance and of his confident expectation of escaping hell-fire. These letters, and indeed most of his extensive writings at this time, throb with religious enthusiasm. They contain sermons on the avoidance of sin, dire warnings of what befalls transgressors, and throughout they are studded with biblical references and quotations. He was constantly reading, too, and praying.

Was he sincere?

Whether he was or not, he was certainly impressive. Everard wrote: 'It cannot indeed be denied that the mind of Holloway, formed as it was by the professors of Christ, is not one of an ordinary stamp, and that, in fact, it displays an energy possessed by few.'

But can we believe this rapid conversion? Is the practised seducer to be believed when he gives advice to women who, he says, encompass their own ruin? Perhaps he does now believe. Perhaps he is now converted.

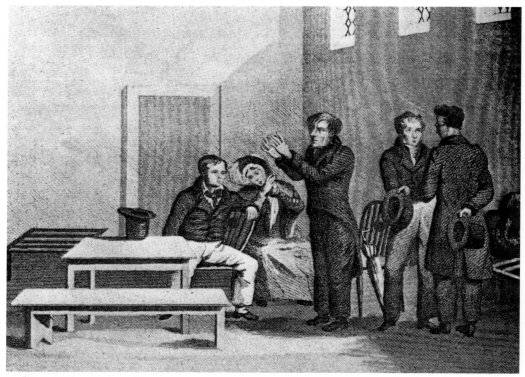

In the infirmary at Horsham Gaol Holloway sits with his mother in another work by J. Perez. His constant supporter, William Nute, is speaking to them.

Holloway next asked if he might see Ann Kennett. He wanted a meeting arranged so that he could persuade her to reveal all she knew.

Ann was conveyed from Lewes to Horsham Gaol. When they met in front of the magistrates, her first words were, 'Oh, John, to what have you brought me?'

But 'in language most energetic' and 'calling on God, before whom he was so shortly to appear, to aid him in his persuasions, to induce her compliance', he begged her to tell the magistrates the full tale.

At this, Ann rounded on him, hitting the table violently and calling him 'deceptive wretch', 'villain', and 'blackguard'. Did he not know she was innocent, she asked. The devil had possessed Holloway, she declared, and he was trying to ruin her.

Holloway swore that he loved her but, 'if she did not disclose all she knew, he could not appease the wrath of Heaven; how could he hope for forgiveness of his crimes if he left the world in ignorance of the facts which were yet undiscovered and he again urged her to reveal all she knew'.

But the woman continued to abuse him, to deny there was anything to tell.

What was Holloway after? Are there signs here of incipient religious mania? Or was he simply a religious humbug, the ultimate betrayer? Ann Kennett's view was that he did not wish her to escape to marry someone else.

Or was there really something else to reveal?

The matter was never very enthusiastically pursued, but a hammer had been found among Ann Kennett's possessions. It had been borrowed from a neighbour and never returned. It had been washed and scraped clean.

Washed of blood? Perhaps so, for it was among some bloody rags found in the High Street lodgings.

Had Holloway told the full truth about the murder? Did Ann help him despatch Celia? He said that she had pulled the cord round the neck. But supposing the real truth was that when he had called Ann to help him, she had come out of the cupboard with a hammer. There had been a bruise on Celia's forehead.

Despite Holloway's pleading that she should tell all she knew, the hammer was never mentioned at the Horsham meeting.

And so they parted. They would not meet again until the trial: they would never again exchange words. The magistrates, for their part, received a poor impression of Kennett. Where Holloway had been calm, she had been violent and rowdy. Not that this was evidence of her guilt.

Holloway's third confession is a curious mangled document in which he tried to confuse matters. There were two Ann Kennetts, he wrote. One of them, but not the one in custody, had helped him murder Celia. The authorities needed to find her and release the Ann Kennett now held in Lewes.

Nearer to the trial, however, Holloway confirmed in a letter to the magistrates that he now stood by his second confession. He wished to bring 'none but the guilty to justice but since that I have let that love which I have toward her overrule me and I have, out of pity to her life, tried to throw a veil over the real truth, and as far as I could, screen her from justice. This, I am sorry to say, I have done against the powerful workings of my own conscience but cannot any longer contain myself till the real truth is known. My first and second statement is truth.'

Ann Kennett as she appeared at Holloway's trial, drawn by J. Perez.

He had thereby condemned Ann Kennett.

So what may we believe? Did Ann Kennett play a greater part in the murder than we have been told?

At Lewes Assizes on 15 December 1831, before Mr Justice Patteson, John Holloway and Ann Kennett faced a charge of murder.

At times Ann was tearful; she fainted; she had to be physically supported; at one point she had to be taken out of the courtroom.

But Holloway, dressed for the occasion in his sailor's clothing, was ferocious.

On his way into court, a small boy, a bystander, had pointed the prisoner out. He could recognise Holloway, he said. Before his escorts could restrain him, Holloway had hit the boy in the face. It was in that fierce mood that the court met him.

At the outset he insisted that the charges be read a second time.

'I don't understand a word of it,' he said.

He was aggressive, arrogant, challenging, angry.

When it was repeated, he shouted fiercely, 'I am not guilty of all that that paper charges me with.'

Asked how he pleaded, he replied 'with utmost ferocity' that he was not guilty until the case was proved against him.

What a contrast with the zealous, contrite, prayerful man of recent months. Perhaps a paragon had been expected in the courtroom at Lewes.

Not so.

Whenever he had the opportunity, he challenged witnesses, refuting their statements in a hostile fashion.

But it was all too strong, the case against him. He railed against all those responsible for his being there, Celia's family and the Overseers at Ardingly who all those years ago had tricked him into marrying. It was they who had brought him to this pass. They were the villains.

At least he told the court that Ann Kennett was innocent, that whatever part she had played was because he had forced her. She was dismissed early in the proceedings. The judge opined that she was not guilty of murder. It was and is astonishing.

The trial lasted a day. Holloway was found guilty.

New charges of being an accessory after the fact were to be brought against her.

Celia's memorial tablet in the churchyard wall of St Peter's in Preston. Note the error – she was murdered in Donkey Row and buried in Lovers' Walk. (The author)

Holloway was hanged at Horsham on Friday 21 December 1831. In the morning he took the sacrament. On the scaffold he went down on his knees to pray. He kissed the Bible, exhorted the crowd of two thousand to mend their ways, and left this life.

After the body had hung a little while, a labourer from Cowfold climbed up on to the staging. He had an unsightly wen on his forehead. Could he have it touched by the dead man, he asked. He could. Holloway's wrists were untied for this. And a handkerchief was placed on the still sweaty chest of the dead man. Dead man's sweat, a sovereign cure.

Two women seeking similar favours of the hangman were sent packing.

Holloway's corpse was returned by coach to Brighton. For twenty-four hours it was exhibited at the Town Hall, where 23,000 men, women and children came to wonder at it. The body was then removed to the hospital for dissection.

In March, Ann Kennett, a mother now, appeared at Lewes Assizes, her baby in her arms. She was charged as an accessory after the fact. The proceedings were brief. She was discharged. She had convinced a judge and jury of her innocence.

Where she went is not known. She was not likely to be found in those turbulent, bawling streets where she and Holloway had set up house for some few months. Even that grim place could never accept so stained a woman, for Holloway's crime was her crime. Ann Kennett must have sought some other haven, some other identity.

Some things linger in the mind. Sometimes, trying to work out what kind of man this Holloway was, one remembers the admission he made to his mother. It was as well he had been caught, he told her, for had he not been stopped, he might have gone to greater lengths. And we think yet again about Sarah Sanders.

In a letter to William Nute, his loyal former employer, Holloway expressed the hope that he would meet Celia in glory. Is that really what he hoped and expected?

On another occasion, when he admitted to having beaten Ann Kennett black and blue, to having torn the hair out of her head, he had confessed that he had done this 'for what reason I do not know. It was my savage nature.'

Holloway's 'savage nature' – what else might it have been responsible for?

5

FAGAN'S LAST CASE

Ringmer, 1838

Perhaps the post was not exciting enough. Perhaps that is why Francis Fagan did not stay longer than sixteen months. He had come to the newly formed East Sussex Constabulary on 22 December 1840 but by 22 March 1842 he, and on the following day his son, also a constable, had handed in their resignations. Of course Superintendent Fagan had worked in London, where the offences were generally more varied. Lewes, where Fagan was based as Superintendent in charge of B Division, encompassed Alfriston, Hailsham, Chailey, Eastbourne, Cuckfield and Ditchling. It was a wide enough area for him, his sergeant and his ten or so constables to cover, but the kinds of offences he dealt with perhaps did not have the thrill about them that he had previously experienced. What was there here to compare with the Metropolitan force to which he had transferred as Inspector after service with the Bow Street Foot Patrol? These country places were tame: some sheep-stealing, barn-breaking, some petty theft, a few assaults. Perhaps that is why Fagan resigned. Perhaps the job lacked excitement. After all, he seems to have been highly regarded. Less than three weeks earlier, he had completed his investigation of a baffling case, one that today might have the tabloids headlining it as 'The Ringmer Vicarage Pond Sex Murder Mystery'. There is no indication anywhere that the magistrates felt that he had failed. The *Sussex Express* reported in October 1841 when the case was before the magistrates, 'Much praise is due to Superintendent Fagan for his indefatigable exertions in this business, and we understand that it is entirely through him that the present inquiry has been instituted.' Possibly the way in which the case turned out later at the Assizes disappointed some, and it may be that this caused the Superintendent to turn his back on East Sussex. The Ringmer case was certainly difficult, and some might have felt that it had not been properly pursued. But this is speculation, nothing more. Sad, though, if it was Fagan's last case which led him to leave the county.

In May 1841 Fagan had received an anonymous letter referring to a 43-year-old woman who had been found drowned at Ringmer in June 1838. The circumstances were unusual and no one had been charged with any offence despite some casual investigation by the local parish constable. An inquest had brought in an open verdict of 'found drowned', and since then there had been no attempt to establish

The record of Francis Fagan's enrolment in Bow Street in 1825. (Courtesy of the Metropolitan Police)

what had happened. Perhaps since his arrival Francis Fagan had heard of the case, but it cannot have crossed his mind that it would be so abruptly resurrected. The broad facts of what had occurred were outlined in the letter which ended 'Take notice. Take the parties where you can find them. The Ringmer people can testify that they were in the woman's company. Be quiet and you have it all. Let them have no interview with each other. More another time.' Mysterious enough, and the author was never discovered.

What chance did an outsider from London have of bringing to a successful conclusion a case which no one had done anything about for three years? Who would know much about it? And who would be willing to speak about what they knew? Fagan's six months' experience must already have taught him that country folk were not only suspicious of the new-fangled police force but also mistrustful of strangers, surly even to those from neighbouring villages. He might well have ignored the letter. He could have torn it up and thrown it on the fire. Who but the writer would have known that he had refused to take action? That he did not do so suggests that he was ready for the challenge, that he was a man not inclined to shun difficulties.

So where did Fagan find his information? He was the first professional policeman in the district, and he went about his task with more skill and vigour than the old-style parish constable who three years earlier had been responsible for the investigation. Most of those involved, whoever and wherever they were, were still alive and living in the locality; there were villagers, the coroner, the magistrates; there were the four men who at the time of the inquest had been suspected of the murder. Over the succeeding months Fagan pursued his enquiries, riding on horseback from his house in Malling Street to Ringmer, an imposing figure whose plain black uniform frock-coat, stovepipe hat and good-quality boots declared an austere authority. At other times, seeking further information, one or other of his constables was detailed to visit the village, on foot of course, and less well shod than his superior, his heavy, black, police-issue boots made to fit either foot.

Unsurprisingly, time had eroded some memories. In other cases there was a distinct reluctance to help the investigation, a deliberate forgetfulness, an antipathy towards the police felt throughout the country which took many years to eradicate. Nevertheless, the essentials of the case were already known and gradually enough additional information accumulated to convince Fagan that he was on the right track and that he would be able to bring to justice whoever was responsible for the murder of Hannah Smith.

The broad details of the murder, if that is what it was, were already well enough known. Early in the morning of 2 June 1838, William Smith had seen off his common-law wife, Hannah Devonshire (known as Smith), from their home in Lewes. A hawker, she travelled all over the county, visiting markets, fairs and racecourses, selling cheap trinkets, tapes, laces, children's novelties. Sometimes she went to villages, few of which offered the kinds of objects that she carried and which were so attractive to her unsophisticated customers. This morning, with ten shillings' worth of goods, she made for Ringmer, her basket over her arm and a new pack containing rags slung across her shoulders.

Hannah had already made some sales when at nine o'clock she arrived at Elizabeth Stephen's beer shop in Ringmer. Here, her day's drinking began and she almost immediately found a drinking companion, the 56-year-old, quaintly named farm labourer General Washer, whose father's one-time service in the militia had influenced the naming of his son. Washer was with Hannah Smith for much of the day. Together they drank beer and ate eels at the beer shop until the early afternoon before moving on to The Green Man. At about eight in the evening they called at The Anchor, where they were joined by Charles Briggs, a labourer, Stephen Stedman, a whitesmith, and John Pockney, a blacksmith, all three in their twenties. The party drank on until eleven o'clock, when Ann Stanford, the landlady, decided that it was time to close. Remarkably, Mrs Stanford thought that Hannah Smith left the pub very steadily despite what had been a fourteen-hour drinking session. 'You are afraid, are you not?' Mrs Stanford had asked her as the hawker stepped out into the night. The road to Lewes at that time of night could be dangerous. 'No, I'm not afraid. I have been on the road too many times. No one will hurt me.' Hannah Smith's last recorded words. Was she really sober? Can she have been?

It was half-past six the following morning when John Gaston went across to the pond behind the vicarage where he was employed as gardener. He wanted water for the garden but saw how trodden down was the grass under the willows. Six feet from the pond he noticed an umbrella and a basket. And, looking now more closely at the water, he thought that there was something below the surface. It was a body, he was sure. He ran for help.

Gaston found three other men, who went back to the pond with him. One of them, Samuel Williams, instantly recognised the basket and umbrella by the side of the pond. They belonged to Hannah Smith, he told the others. She had sold some items to him only the day before. The body lay in eight feet of water but together, using a rake and a long pole, the men brought it to the bank and removed the

Ringmer Vicarage, drawn by John Harding.

pack that was still slung across the dead woman's shoulders. Although it must have been apparent to them that she was dead, they tried to rub some life into the corpse. They even sent to The Anchor for brandy in the hope that they might revive her.

The four men, now joined by Henry Weller, the parish constable, stood puzzling how the woman had come to die in such a fashion. They were naturally interested in such a dramatic event, in which they had played so important a part. There was damage to one of the willow trees growing out of the water at the pond's edge, and they wondered if she had slipped down the steeply sloping sides and tried unsuccessfully to snatch at it as she fell towards the water. They speculated. Could she have just fallen in the pond? Might she have been pushed?

Wandering around the pond, the men came across the footprints of three or four people. The imprints were distinct as there had been a heavy dew. With some enthusiasm they followed the track but it petered out, at which point their detective work came to an abrupt halt.

Within a short time word was out that a body had been brought out of the pond, and several people gathered to view the corpse lying by the sloping bankside. Among them was General Washer. The idea of a 'scene of crime' did not then exist, so that the viewers plodded around, destroying whatever useful information there might have been, though in truth no parish constable would have known how to read whatever signs there were. But there was some information which was significant. Hannah Smith's basket contained only a little wooden box valued at a penny and two tin pots worth twopence each. Had she sold the rest of her wares? Later in the day, when the story reached a wider audience, there would be those who would wonder how she could have sold so much when she was drinking most of the day.

Eventually, the body was taken in a wheelbarrow to a shed belonging to a neighbouring house. When Dr Gray arrived at the scene he did not thoroughly examine the body, expecting that he would be called to the coroner's court, where he would make a more detailed examination. He noticed, however, that there were no marks of violence on the upper part of the body.

In the afternoon the inquest was held at The Anchor, where less than twenty-four hours earlier Hannah Smith had drunk her time away. William Smith, who attended the inquest, was surprised to note the few articles in her basket, especially as there was no money found on her person. It looked like robbery. It might even be murder. But in the circumstances, 'Found drowned' was about the best verdict the coroner's jury could reach.

The day after the inquest Hannah Smith was buried in Ringmer churchyard. The coroner had decreed that the matter be left open for further investigation if necessary. It was never anticipated that such an investigation would take place. Nor would it have done had not Superintendent Fagan received the anonymous letter.

In the weeks following the inquest there had been an investigation of sorts. Public suspicion had pointed at Washer and the three young men. It might be said that nothing resulted from the enquiries, though some might have questioned Stephen Stedman's almost immediate departure from the village. Then shortly after Fagan began his enquiry, John Pockney had left for Ramsgate. In a letter to a friend he said that he left the village because he had been 'too fond of company' and was in debt. But another reason was that people 'talked about a certain matter'. Fagan's questions had had an almost instant effect.

After patient investigation, Fagan arrested General Washer on 11 October, charging him with murder. He had learnt that sometime after midnight on the night of Hannah Smith's death he had been seen in the village. Furthermore, Washer had a conviction for violence against a woman. Three years earlier, while drunk, he had attacked the wife of the licensee at The Green Man.

On 14 October at the County Hall in Lewes General Washer was examined by the magistrates, the Earl of Chichester in the chair. So that Pockney, Briggs and Stedman could have no warning of how far the investigation had progressed, the first of the two days of the proceedings was not made public. On the second day, however, when the examination was resumed, the press were allowed full access to the court. Oddly, the Briggs family, rather than Washer, came under the spotlight.

John Briggs, who lived near the pond, told the court that he remembered the night Hannah Smith was drowned. So he should. It was to his shed that her body was taken when it was retrieved and there that Dr Gray performed his perfunctory examination. After this initial admission, however, Briggs was unable to assist the court.

Both of his sons, Charles and Joseph, had been out that night, he said, but he was unable to say which of them came home first. He had been asleep. Nor could he remember if they got up before he did the following morning, Saturday, but he did not see them all that day. He was also uncertain when he heard that Charles was being mentioned in connection with the murder, even though it was the talk of the village. To the unconcealed surprise of the Earl of Chichester, Briggs was even unsure if he had asked Charles whether he had had anything to do with it. Nor could he bring to mind whether he had talked to him about it.

The Briggs brothers were no clearer in their recollection of events. Joseph had gone to Lewes to fetch medicine for his mother. He had returned home, he thought, at about eleven o'clock, but he could not be sure. When he arrived home he had asked his mother if Charles had returned and she had said that he had. But he was unable to say with any certainty which of them was first in bed, even though they shared the same bed. Astonishingly, Joseph could not remember whether he had heard that his brother and Stedman were suspected. He said that he did not hear of the matter until the Saturday night, which is breathtakingly difficult to believe as Hannah Smith's body had been in the shed in the morning and the whole mysterious business was the talk of the village. And no, even though he knew Stedman well enough – he lived only a couple of hundred yards away – Joseph could not recall him leaving the village.

Charles Briggs had an equally imperfect memory of that night. He said that he, Pockney and Stedman left The Anchor soon after eleven o'clock. He went straight home and the other two went towards Lewes. He did not remember his brother Joseph coming home but thought he was already in bed. He could not say for certain when Joseph came home. 'I always thought he was in bed before me; he says he was in bed after me.' Most telling, however, he could remember that Washer and Hannah Smith were still drinking when he and the other two left.

What shines through the testimonies of the Briggs' family is their evident determination not to incriminate each other. Their answers were evasive, even conflicting at times, but they gave away nothing, apart from Charles trying to leave the impression that General Washer might be involved.

The Anchor, 2005. (The author)

For his part, Washer, now nearing sixty, the prospect of the gallows before him, vehemently denied that he had stayed at The Anchor after the others had left. 'I never saw the woman after I left her at The Anchor,' Washer said. 'I am satisfied it won't be me to suffer and I hope those who hurt her will not close their eyelids before they are found out. It hasn't disturbed me in the least yet but to suffer innocently is a hard case.'

Washer said that he had never met Hannah Smith before 2 June. He agreed that after leaving The Anchor he had been out at midnight but, as he explained, it was a fine summer's night and he had gone outside for a smoke. But he knew nothing else of the affair. And yes, of course he had turned up at the pond to look at the body when it was retrieved from the water, but he was not alone in that. It was nothing but curiosity that took him there, just as the drowning had attracted others.

Another witness appeared who also cast some doubt on Washer's innocence. Jane Sexton, who lived in the village, said that about two years earlier, in 1840 perhaps, she and Washer had tried on each other's spectacles and found that they could both see better if they made an exchange. But William Smith said that the spectacles produced in court by Mrs Sexton were those worn by Hannah when she left home for the last time. He would have recognised them anywhere. They had been repaired at home in a rough and ready fashion, just as these were. But then while they probably had belonged to Hannah Smith, they could easily have been exchanged during the day's drinking, just as they had been several months later.

While Washer continued to protest his innocence – 'I am as innocent as the day I was born. I wish I had no more accounts to take up than that' – the court was less than convinced, and he was charged with murder and committed to stand trial at the next Assizes.

In the very week when Washer was appearing before the magistrates the *Sussex Express* observed that 'for several weeks past an inquiry of the most searching character has been carried on by the magistrates of the Lewes bench and the police, under the direction of Superintendent Fagan'.

Fagan had learnt that Stephen Stedman was now living in Watford, and travelled there to arrest him. Here, on 21 October, he found a man whose recent behaviour had been irreproachable and who was on the point of being married. His employer in Watford for the past sixteen months would later state that if Stedman were proved innocent he would willingly employ him again.

Until now Stedman had thought that the episode of three years earlier was forgotten. The sudden appearance of a policeman charging him with murder was devastating. He was deeply distressed, stating 'bad company had brought him to it'. Together, presumably handcuffed, the two men returned to Lewes, although they could not complete the journey in one day. 'I then brought him to London where we slept in a double-bedded room,' Fagan told the magistrates later, 'and as soon as he got into bed he wept very much and then made a statement.'

The following is the statement as it appeared some weeks later in the *Sussex Express*. In that shabby London lodging house where they stayed – the lodging allowance for a prisoner was only ninepence a day – Fagan listened to this confession and probably wrote down a version almost immediately but it was most likely revised for grammar and spelling and expression on their return to Lewes.

Stedman admitted to being involved in the affair of the woman who was drowned. Pockney, he said, had arranged for them all to have intercourse with her.

> She appeared in liquor. We had some beer together. Pockney went out first and had some conversation with the woman. Briggs and I followed. Pockney and the woman went into the field where he abused her person. The deceased was so tipsy that she was not aware what was going on. I then went to her and committed the same offence and afterwards became dreadfully alarmed. Briggs then went and violated her. Pockney and Briggs then assaulted her and violated her. Pockney and Briggs then assaulted her a second time and then began to rifle her pockets. I don't know what was taken but did not see any money. I proposed getting her into the road but we eventually agreed to leave her in the field. We left her asleep and proceeded with the basket to the churchyard and divided the contents. We then returned the basket, leaving it beside her, laying the umbrella across it and went home. There was a great stir in the village the next morning, and I became much alarmed, and, to avoid detection, burnt all the articles stolen and recommended Pockney to do the same. I immediately left Ringmer and proceeded round the country and eventually reached Watford, Herts, where the officer apprehended me.

It was as a consequence of Stedman's arrest that John Pockney was arrested in Brighton. At the Superintendent's house he made a statement, admitting he was with Hannah Smith on the night of her death. Charles Briggs, arrested at his Ringmer home, was less cooperative, at one point remaining silent for half an hour before admitting to being at The Anchor with the others.

On 26 and 28 October the men appeared before the magistrates at Lewes on a double charge of murder and larceny. 'Pockney and Briggs', said the *Sussex Express*, 'had the appearance of decent labouring men.' Stedman, dressed in a black suit, appeared very alarmed by his situation. He was clearly ill and was accommodated in a chair throughout the examination. Only Charles Briggs and his father, John, appear to have stood up for themselves, facing up to the Earl of Chichester with a continued failure to recall any precise details of the night of 2 June. Charles, questioning some of the witnesses who had dragged the body from the pond, managed to have their agreement that Hannah Smith in her drunken state might well have stumbled down the steep bank and into the pond.

All three accused were now committed for trial at the Assizes, charged with murder and larceny. It passed almost unnoticed that in November General Washer was bailed and that shortly afterwards, without any fanfares, the case against him was dropped.

On 3 March 1842 the Grand Jury concluded that the charges of murder could not be proceeded with. There was insufficient evidence of murder against the accused, and their statements could not be used against each other. Instead they were to be charged with assault and theft. The trial then began, Lord Alderson presiding.

There was of course an assault by the defence on the statements the men were alleged to have made. The tussle over the statements was in fact the nub of the case. How had Fagan managed to persuade Briggs, Pockney and Stedman to make them? Were they under pressure? What threats, what promises were made? What lies were told them? That was the defence line, for if the statements could be demolished then there would be no case for the men to answer.

Fagan, cross-examined by Mr Sergeant Shea, denied telling Stedman that it would be better for him to tell him all about it. 'I never said to the prisoner that if he were admitted evidence [as a witness for the prosecution] I would get him a situation at Mr Cubitt's.'

Stedman's statement had undergone a change since his tearful confession in London. Perhaps he believed that his forthcoming marriage would be imperiled if he stuck by the original. Now it stated 'that he being unfortunately one of those who were connected in the disgraceful affair of the woman who was drowned, he considered it his duty to appease his conscience by divulging that which he knew about it. The unfortunate woman was sitting in the taproom when he went in The Anchor. Pockney having told him that he had made it all right with the old woman, they went into the field and had connections with her. He [Stedman] most strongly denied that he had any connection with her but confessed to having taken some of the articles.' It concluded by stating it was 'The truth, the whole truth, and nothing but the truth, so help me God.' A further confession of Stedman was then read, but contained nothing material, and he again most solemnly declared that he had no connection with the deceased on the night in question.'

And Pockney's statement? Mr Chambers for Pockney cross-examined Fagan. What tricks had the policeman employed in his client's case? 'I was not present at the time when the statement was made,' Fagan said, 'but I read it at the station house when he signed it. I do not remember having any specific conversation with him. I never told Pockney that the other parties had confessed. I never used the word "splitting" to him. I never made any promise or threatened him before he signed it.'

Pockney's statement admitted that he, Briggs and Stedman were talking with Hannah Smith in The Anchor at about eleven o'clock on the night of her death. The men agreed among themselves to have intercourse with her.

I went out first, when the deceased came out, and I spoke to her and she said she had no objection. Stedman and Briggs followed behind me. I took her into the fields. When she laid down, I had connection with her. Briggs went next and Stedman next. I went a second time. I don't recollect who put their hands into her pocket. I had the work-box; Stedman had a snuff-box and some other little articles. We shared the things in the churchyard. Stedman then went home. On the following morning when I got up General Washer called me out, and said, 'Where did you leave the old woman last night, because she's dead, and I thought you might have had some nonsense with her.' I said I couldn't stop now as I was in a hurry.

Ringmer churchyard, 2005. (Alan Skinner)

Pockney's confession further stated that after the inquest he and Stedman agreed to burn the items they had stolen. 'Stedman told me that he had thrown something into the pond at the back of his brother's house,' Pockney's statement continues. 'We left the woman near the pond asleep. I don't know anything about the spectacles.'

A further statement by Pockney was also read. 'Before we left I said she was asleep. Briggs said, "Let us see what she's got in her basket," and then he took something out of her basket. Stedman then took a snuff box out of the deceased's pocket.'

Fagan claimed that in October Briggs had made a statement to the following effect: 'I went into the Anchor and saw the woman in the house. Stedman, Pockney and Washer were there. We left about 11 o'clock. I only saw deceased drink a glass of ale. Pockney went on with the deceased, and Stedman and myself followed. He then stated to having connection with the poor woman, and sharing the articles in the churchyard, leaving the deceased asleep near the pond.'

Now Briggs, stubborn as he had been previously, was proclaiming his innocence. Although he admitted to being with the others, he denied having had 'connection' with Hannah Smith; neither had he assaulted her nor had he stolen her belongings. Before the closing speeches were made the judge observed, 'I don't see any case against Charles Briggs, excluding as I do, all the confessions made by the other prisoners.' An odd and quirky kind of judgment, one might say. But at the time a prisoner could not be convicted solely on the evidence of his accomplices in a crime.

Briggs had pleaded not guilty to the charges and the only evidence against him came from Pockney and Stedman. Fortunate Briggs, despicable Briggs, who had earlier tried to cast the blame on General Washer, one of his neighbours.

Summing up, the judge remarked that it was not fair to assume that the deceased came by her death in any unfair way. He thought it very probable that being drunk she had staggered into the pond. He cautioned the jury that the confession of Pockney should not in the slightest degree affect Stedman and vice versa.

John Pockney and Stephen Stedman were both found guilty of larceny. Pockney was sentenced to two years' hard labour and Stedman to eighteen months. But perhaps this was a light sentence. Pockney's account suggests that after Hannah Smith's agreement to go with the three of them it turned into what today would surely be classified as a gang-rape.

But how did Hannah Smith die? Did the court hear the truth? Did Hannah Smith, on the edge of the pond, sleeping off beer and excessive 'connection' with three men, simply slip down the bank and into the water? Or did something more sinister, something more wicked, occur?

The answer may lie in the pack which Hannah Smith was carrying on her back when she was fished out of the water. When she lay down on the grass prior to intercourse she must have removed the pack from her shoulders, if not for her own comfort and convenience, then for the sake of her clients.

After it is over, she, raped, and her basket looted of its tawdry trinkets, the men go. She lies sleeping. When she awakens, minutes or hours later, she staggers to her feet, still in a drunken haze. Her pack is on the ground beside her and she pulls it on. But she is uncertain on her feet, unable to keep her balance, staggering, slipping on the dewy grass. And then she stumbles, slides down the steep bank, reaches out and grabs a willow branch which does not halt her progress, and falls into the water. Her thick, wide skirts serve to keep her afloat so that for seconds, no more than seconds, she moves along the surface of the water, thrashing her arms until she sinks. That would seem to be what really happened at the pond at Ringmer. And that is another explanation for the death of the 'old woman'. Even General Washer had referred to her as 'the old woman', and so had Stedman. But the fact remains that her end might not have been like that. *Did she slip or was she pushed?*

There is another matter which cannot be cleared up. Why, almost immediately after an investigation which, on the face of it, was successful, did Francis Fagan give up his well-paid post – £140 per annum – and leave Lewes? Years earlier he had been a stonemason. Did he want to return to a more precise, less complicated trade? There is no record of his return to the Metropolitan police force. Was his departure in any way connected with the Ringmer affair? Were his masters dissatisfied with the case he had brought before the court? Had he in some way failed? Or did he tire of the tameness of Sussex? Was that all it was?

6

ALL FOR A ROLL OF CARPET

Brighton, 1844

They flock here, the noblemen, the landed gentry, the substantial professional classes, the comfortable tradesfolk. They are dedicated followers of fashion, some of them, attracted by celebrity, by the notion of the new; they come to Brighton because that is what people do in the 1840s. That may be unkind. They are not all like that. Many come for the Theatre Royal; for the Assembly Rooms; for the baths, churches, inns. They come for that wonder of the new age, the Chain Pier; for the reading rooms; the entertainments; for the Pump Room. And it is healthy, this town of 47,000 souls, no doubt about that, though hard on the purse. Even so, some can afford to live in the elegant crescents which look out over the Channel.

Some years ago, Count Pecchio, a visitor from Milan, summed it up in a letter home:

Houses, food, horses, everything is here even more expensive than in London. But the sky is free from fog and fumes; from October to January Brighton is inhabited only by Dukes and Peers. Here you can see, daily and gratis, a princess of the royal blood, four duchesses, etc. taking their walk.

If lately, since the accession of the young queen, there has been some toning down of the fashionable excesses of the past, here you may still see the beau monde in all its elegant bad taste, its fastidious carelessness, its painstaking nonchalance. It will do anything to catch the eye.

But on the other side of the Steine, only a few hundred yards from the fine squares and terraces of this exquisite spa town, in ugly contrast to the gracious crescents, is a squalid, dark little world. This is the crowded rookery of high-density, low-quality building, of tiny alleys and shadowy mazes leading off Edward Street.

Here are workmen's cottages, lodging houses, little workshops, jerry-built tenements, beershops. It is a random world. The constables are constantly called out here to the disturbances, to resolve brawls, domestic upheavals, petty offences. Here, a stroll away from the Royal Pavilion, live unskilled men, hawkers, journeymen, craftsmen, farm labourers, fishermen, out-of-works, drunks, ne'er-do-wells, chancers, women on the game, full- or part-time. It is a shifting, unsettled population. These streets, courts, alleyways, are 'an intolerable nuisance to the town at large', according to Dr Jenks's report to the Poor Law Commissioners. 'They are the resort of tramps, begging imposters and prostitutes of the lowest description.' Strange contrasts in this town: squalor and extravagance, wealth and abject poverty, respectability and earnestness alongside vice of the most wanton kind.

And here, in this suspect quarter of the town, at The Globe in Edward Street, is John Lawrence, drinking away this whole March day, as he has drunk away the two previous days. There is some uncertainty about this young man's age. He is an old-looking twenty-four, but that is the age he claims to be. Not that it much matters. A curious observer might wonder why it is that such a good-looking fellow, clearly strong, well spoken and 'of genteel appearance', should be passing so much of his time in taprooms like this. Why is he not at work? Why is he not looking after his family?

John Lawrence, murderer of Henry Solomon, and the last felon to hang at Horsham.

The truth is that John Lawrence has somehow let his family down. His mother must have had the highest expectations of him, for the family was very respectable. He had been brought up in Tunbridge Wells and later at Speldhurst, where his step-father had a smallholding. Some years earlier he had been apprenticed to his father as a plasterer but had not completed his indentures. Later he had worked for his uncle, selling water in parts of Tunbridge Wells where the water supply was inadequate. But he had given up this work and had gone to work on the Brighton railway. But again he gave up the job. From then it was a predictable, downward spiral, with companions as feckless as he was proving himself to be, drinking heavily, hoping that he could get by from one day to the next. Then it was gaol in Maidstone, apparently serving three sentences, once for the theft of a leg of mutton, a second time more seriously for passing base coin and for some unspecified offence on a third occasion. Although it is not certain, it may be that this sentence followed a brawl in a pub where he was working as a potboy. In the struggle with a workmate, he had stabbed him in the cheek. John Lawrence is a dangerous man, and today he is in drink.

Lawrence has been in Brighton for some hours on the day when we meet him drinking in The Globe. It is said that six months earlier he left Speldhurst with money stolen from his stepfather, though the police are unaware of this. But the police wonder about him, because he looks very like someone who has been seen in the last three or four months hanging around houses later broken into. Certainly he consorts with thieves. And with gamblers, too, and is considered to be 'a sure card', and he scrapes a few pence this way from time to time. At present Lawrence is pimp to a girl known as 'Hastings Bett'. He lives with her though he is of no fixed abode, this man brought up so carefully in a steady home. Bett, it seems, maintains him. It is her regular work that allows him his beer money, although his present three-day drinking binge has only been made possible by selling or pawning some of her clothes. Not that it is all one-sided, for on occasion he has had to sell and pawn his own rings, too. At nights, to ensure that Bett is safe, he goes out with her. Not that she is absolutely safe from him because only hours earlier he has been obliged to beat her severely when she has complained that he has stolen her jewellery.

But he is not alone in The Globe. He has a companion, a man as dissolute as he is, though we shall never learn his name. Shortly after seven o'clock when they leave the pub, they spot an opportunity. In St James's Street they see a carpet propped up just outside the door of Caleb Collins's shop. It is just the sort of opportunity that any incompetent petty criminal will think about taking. A carpet is difficult to conceal; it is difficult to run with when you have it over your shoulder; it may not be easy to sell. But the two men recently out in the fresh air after hours at The Globe perhaps did not think in that way. There it was, a roll of carpet, just waiting to be picked up. And so they went for it.

Henry Solomon, the Chief Officer of Police, was talking to Samuel Slight, son of the Clerk to the Commissioners, and two others, Edward Butler, the Poor Rate Collector, and William Alger, a draper, in the cramped, little basement police office in the Town Hall when Police Constable Barnden brought Lawrence in. The constable explained that he had been called to Collins's shop in St James's Street. Two men had run off with a carpet valued at £6, and one of them, the man in custody, had been caught in Chapel Street by the shop assistant. The carpet had been recovered. It

Henry Solomon, Chief Officer of Brighton Police.

was the kind of case which came into the office several times a day; there was little to mark it out from countless others. Solomon sent the constable back to the shop to bring in the carpet and took over the questioning of Lawrence.

It might have been thought daunting to be interrogated by such a well-regarded policeman as Henry Solomon. Though he had had no training for his work, would not have understood 'forensics', and had no experience of policing beyond Brighton's boundaries, he had a natural ability for investigating and organising and for understanding the complexities of the task. He had proved himself over the last twenty-three years a loyal and able servant of the Brighton Town Commissioners since he had left his trade as watchmaker in 1821. His duties in those years had been varied. He had been in turn Inspector of Post Horse Duty; Inspector of Hackney Coaches, Bathing Machines and Pleasure Boats; Inspector of Nuisances and Inspector of Gas Lights. Then, in 1838, when the Commissioners had decided to institute a Peel-style police force in place of the 'Charlies', the old-time watchmen, who were no longer capable of maintaining order in the raucous town, they had looked no further than their faithful servant for their first Chief Officer. For the next six years, Solomon proved how excellent a choice the Commissioners had made. His earnest application and his distinct ability won him the praises of magistrates and judges and indeed of the general law-abiding public. And here, in his tiny office, in the early Wednesday evening of 13 March 1844, he sat in his chair facing John Lawrence, a petty criminal. Solomon had faced many John Lawrences. There was nothing to suggest that this John Lawrence would respond any differently from all of the others. There would be the resentfulness, the truculence and then most likely an abject or grudging confession.

What was his name? Solomon asked Lawrence.

'King,' Lawrence answered. Or perhaps he said, 'Smith.' The record is unclear. The witnesses, Slight and Alger and Butler, were paying little attention. Although not policemen, as Town Hall officials they were accustomed to the regular traffic in and out of the police office.

No regular place of abode? Well, where did he sleep the previous night?

'In Darby Place, about halfway down, with a friend.'

Name of his friend?

Lawrence claimed not to know.

How long had he been in Brighton, then?

Brighton Town Hall.
The office in which
Solomon was murdered
was in the basement.

PARTICULARS
OF THE
MURDEROUS ASSAULT
AND
DEATH
OF
Mr SOLOMON
Chief Officer of the
BRIGHTON POLICE.

Just as our paper was being put to press last night, a man was apprehended on suspicion of stealing a piece of carpet from Mr. Collins, St. James's Street, and taken to the Chief Officer's room in the Town Hall. Mr. Solomon was conversing with two or three persons in the room, when the villain, whose name we understand to be Lawrence, slipped round to the fire-place, took up the poker, and aimed a deadly blow at the Chief Officer, which alighted on his head, and felled him to the ground, inflicting a dreadful wound six inches in length. The wound bled profusely; medical aid was immediately called in : the wound was dressed, and the sufferer conveyed to his residence in a very precarious state. His murderous assailant was immediately secured and handcuffed. The fellow had just before asked for a knife, saying that he wanted to cut his own throat. The poker was bent by the force of the blow.

We understand that the prisoner was seen by Mrs. Akhurst, wife of Mr. Akhurst, Grocer, at the corner of the New Steine, to take up a large roll of felt carpet, which was standing outside of Mr. Collins's door, and walk off with it. Mrs. Akhurst gave information at Mr. Collins' shop, and the prisoner was pursued into Chapel Street, and apprehended. On searching the prisoner, the officers found several duplicates for articles which had been pledged in the names of King and Smith. The Surgeon who attended Mr. Solomon at the Hall were Mr. Baldey and Mr. Cordy Burrows; and after he was taken home, Mr. Blaker and another surgeon also attended.

On enquiry at Solomon's residence we learn that little if any hope is entertained of the Chief Officer's recovery. He remains insensible; and is not expected to survive many hours.

The prisoner's name is Lawrence, and he is known amongst his associates by the nick-name of "Mag." He has stated that he comes from Tunbridge Wells, where he was apprenticed to a plasterer. Six years ago he was " in trouble," and on coming out of gaol, he obtained work as a _____ labourer for some time, after which he fell into bad company, and _____ his life has been a burden to him. He states that he bore no enmity against Solomon, and for Solomon's sake is sorry for what he did; but that for his own sake, he should rejoice in hearing that the wound had terminated fatally, as that would give him a prospect of being ridded of his existence. He is about twenty-four years of age; and is dressed in a pepper-and-salt Chesterfield coat, with trowsers of the same material. He states that he has been in Brighton for several months; and although unknown to the police, he knows them and calls them by name. He is secured by hand-cuffs and leg-irons, and an officer is constantly with him in his cell. He bore no appearance of having been drinking, and we understand that he denies that he stole the carpet.

Brighton Gazette, Thursday March 14, 1844.

Further Particulars.
Thursday Morning.

It was ascertained at the Town Hall, at about half-past ten o'clock this Morning, that Mr. Solomon had expired.

The sitting Magistrates assembled at the Town Hall at an earlier hour than usual this morning; the place was soon crowded by persons anxious to hear the particulars of this sudden and horrid murder. The prisoner who appeared much dejected was brought in and placed at the bar, when several most respectable and influential inhabitants of the town, who were present at the time the fatal blow was struck arrived, and upon whose evidence he now stands committed to take his trial for Wilful Murder at the ensuing Assizes.

THE INQUEST.

The Inquest was held at the Town Hall, this day Friday. The Prisoner presented an appearance of perfect indifference, looking around at the persons present, and now and then recognising with a familiar nod some of his former associates. The Jury retired for a short time and returned with a verdict of Wilful Murder against the Prisoner. He was shortly after conveyed to Lewes in a private carriage.

Details of Henry Solomon's murder. This was published on the day after the assault.

At first Lawrence said two days. Then, after further probing and prodding from Solomon, he suggested two weeks. It was not true, of course, and Solomon was probably dubious about this answer.

Then there was an outburst. Lawrence was standing up, pulling off the black stock round his neck. 'It's no good saying anything about it!' he shouted. 'I'm tired of life. Give me a knife and I will murder myself.'

Solomon tried to calm down the agitated man, persuading him to sit quietly in an armchair by the fireplace. Some time after this, Mr Collins, the shopkeeper, came into the office to see if he could identify the prisoner, but he could not.

Other business went on. Others came into the office to speak to Solomon. They seem to have paid little attention to Lawrence, huddled in the armchair by the fire.

Constable Barnden, now returned to the office, was waiting in the passageway for a witness when he heard a shout of 'Police!' from inside.

'I ran into the office and saw Mr Solomon in the act of falling to the floor. Mr Samuel Slight immediately took hold of the prisoner, and I also seized him. I then looked round, and saw Mr Solomon bleeding from the head, and there was blood all over the floor.'

While a doctor was sent for, Barnden and Slight put the cuffs on Lawrence and sat him down once more. Then they fastened leg chains on him.

'I hope I have killed him and that I shall be hung for it,' Lawrence said. 'The first chance I can get I will make off with myself. I looked round to see if I could get a knife but I could not see one,' he added.

It had all happened so suddenly. Solomon had got up from behind his desk and walked over to the fire and then, as he was returning to his seat, Lawrence had seized the poker and had struck him on the right side of the head. Slight had called out for help and had wrested the poker from him.

In the course of the evening Solomon's head wounds were dressed and later he regained consciousness. He asked questions about what had occurred and gave orders that Lawrence was to be charged with assault. Then he was taken home and at about ten o'clock lost consciousness again. He never recovered, and died the following morning.

Taken before the magistrates, Lawrence, heavily ironed and handcuffed, was charged with theft and murder. Some account of his background was given – his home and parents; the efforts of his stepfather to help him; the descent into crime. In the course of the hearing, the chairman of magistrates, Major Allen, referring to the fact that the carpet had been unattended outside the shop, said that it was 'a very improper practice. You see that this temptation has led this unfortunate man into the crime of murder. You should not expose persons in poverty to this temptation.' That his fellow magistrates approved of this sentiment, given Lawrence's history, is unlikely.

Lawrence was invited to make a statement but declined. He was then committed to the House of Correction at Lewes, where he was to await the next Assizes, to be held on 19 March. As he left the court, several people, 'apparently of the lower class', spoke to him, and a young woman, presumably 'Hastings Bett', promised to 'send him a clean shirt'. Overnight in the cells he was apparently in good spirits.

The following afternoon, as he was being conveyed to Lewes, Lawrence remarked on the huge crowds in the street. Perhaps he wondered if they had turned out to see him. After all, not every criminal achieves such notoriety, for a police killing is mercifully rare. But he was disabused of any such illusions. What he was seeing was a funeral, a huge turn-out, people lining the streets, soberly awaiting a funeral cortege. The *Brighton Guardian* describes the scene.

Not less than ten thousand persons were present, anxious to manifest sympathy with those who had thus suddenly, and by the hands of lawless violence, been deprived of their natural protector. The whole of the police force, with Mr Slight at its head, the High Constable, the town Beadles, and a large body of tradesmen were formed in procession, and walking in twos preceded the corpse to its last earthly home. The hearse containing the body was followed by two mourning coaches with the relatives of the deceased and the Reader of the Synagogue; and all the adult members of the Congregation of Jews followed in flies to be present and to assist at the interment. The mournful procession and the mass of the people by whom it was surrounded was set in motion soon after three o'clock, and moved slowly along Grand parade at the Ditchling road; and shortly after 4 o'clock the remains were received at the burial ground and after the performance of the usual service, were lowered into the grave prepared for their reception.

Lawrence questioned the policeman escorting him, 'It is not Mr Solomon's funeral, is it?' And of course it was. And then with a total absence of feeling he said that he thought people foolish to go to such sights. When he was in Maidstone Gaol there were two executions but he had gone to neither. And so the journey went on, Lawrence discussing horse-racing and other matters while in Brighton thousands acknowledged the passing of a fine Chief Officer of Police.

The Brighton Town Commissioners' minutes of 20 March 1844, so shortly after the murder, read,

Henry Solomon's gravestone.

It is with the most painful feelings the Commissioners have heard the awful account of the wilful murder of Mr Henry Solomon, Chief Officer of the Police, and commend the Clerk for the steps he has taken in bringing the Murderer to justice. The Commissioners cannot but express in strongest terms their abhorrence and detestation of this cold-blooded deed, which has deprived the town of an old faithful and valuable servant, the country of a most zealous and vigilant officer, and a mother and nine children of the only support on which they had depended for subsistence.

At Lewes, John Lawrence appeared before Lord Chief Justice Denman. His counsel could not put up any persuasive defence and he was condemned to death by a jury which did not leave the jury box. The jury and all of the witnesses donated their fees to Solomon's wife and nine children.

Transferred to Horsham for execution, Lawrence was apparently remorseful and when he met his brother he adjured him to mend his ways.

John Lawrence was the last man to be publicly executed in Horsham. At noon on Easter Saturday, 6 April 1844, the day of Horsham Teg Fair, a crowd of over 3000 turned out to watch his 'turning off'. Many of course came this day for the traditional annual signing-on as farm hands and hedgers, dairymaids, cowmen and shepherds, but others were doubtless drawn to the town solely by the prospect of a hanging. Despite the best efforts of the clergy in their Good Friday sermons to calm down the populace, despite their efforts to persuade schoolmasters to march their scholars up Denne Park, out of the way, so that they should not witness the scene, many children and women were present to see Lawrence's exit.

For centuries most executions in Sussex had been carried out in public at Horsham, a town of only 2,700 inhabitants. Horsham 'Hang Fair' had always attracted large crowds and there were especially many on this occasion, as there had been no hangings in the town in the past eight years.

The gallows was erected at the west front of the county gaol which faced Denne Park. Everywhere in the vicinity of the gaol were throngs of people, many of whom had come from long distances. It was said that the brother Lawrence had advised to mend his ways turned up drunk and boasting that he was an even greater scoundrel than the condemned man.

There was a carnival air about the event, a general sense of callous levity. The owner of a beer-shop was heard to say that he wished there was a hanging every day, for trade was so good. Gingerbread sellers and piemen, sellers of combs and lace, called out their wares. Beggars pleaded for odd change and while they did not advertise their presence, pickpockets found enough to occupy themselves in the dense mob. One of the several Brighton orange sellers was heard shouting out, 'If any man says I'm idle, let him wield this truck of oranges up from Brighton. These are beautiful oranges. They'll melt like butter, run down your throat like a wheelbarrow; they're sugar outside, brandy in the middle, and the rind will make you good boot soles.'

The ballad sellers as usual on such occasions had their crudely sentimental, ready-made verses at a penny a sheet. One of these bestsellers was entitled 'The Mother – to Her Condemned Son'.

Another highly popular one reads:

> Good people all, I pray draw near,
> A dreadful story you shall hear:
> Overcome with grief and fear,
> I am condemned to die.
> I do lament, and sore repent,
> The evil deed which I have done;
> My time is come, my glass is run,
> I now behold my setting sun – all in the prime of life.
>
> John Lawrence is my name,
> To grief and shame,
> I brought myself this world may see,
> Young men a warning take by me,
> At Horsham, on a fatal tree,
> Alas! I am doomed to die.

Even so, in spite of the general excitement and drunkenness, the police reinforcements all the way from London, who patrolled the town, reported no serious incidents.

At twelve o'clock Lawrence appeared, his arms tied behind his back. He mounted the gallows, described as 'a ghastly affair of timber and canvas, both painted black'.

Sussex County Gaol, Horsham, drawn by Henry Burstow, who was present at Lawrence's execution. The cross designates the position of the gallows.

APPEAL
FOR THE WIDOW AND NINE CHILDREN OF MR. HENRY SOLOMON.

HENRY SOLOMON was for more than twenty years in public employment, and a great part of the time Chief Officer of Police in Brighton. He fell in the prime of life, on the 13th inst., whilst discharging his public duties, a victim to the murderous attack of a ruthless assassin; thus producing, in the emphatic language of the Chief Justice of England, in His Lordship's charge to the Grand Jury, "the death of a most courageous, intelligent, active, and humane officer, and a most serious loss to the public and his family." It is for this family, consisting of a widow and nine children utterly destitute, that the joint Committees appointed by the town and the Commissioners make this most urgent appeal for pecuniary aid to the sympathy of the public, and especially to all who as inhabitants or visitors may permanently or occasionally have resided at Brighton. The Committees are encouraged by the spirit of liberality already shewn (for which they on behalf of the family tender their grateful thanks) to hope that they may be enabled to carry out the objects expressed by the unanimous resolutions passed at the meetings, and make a permanent provision for the widow and children, either by sinking the amount contributed in the purchase of an annuity for the life of the widow, or, in case it should be sufficiently large, by investing it in the names of trustees, to pay the interest to the widow, and expend the principal in the permanent advancement of the children, by which means can be best supplied the great loss they have sustained in the cruel destruction of their natural protector.

Subscriptions will be received at the Brighton Banks, by the Honorary Secretary, at the Clerk's Office, Town Hall, and by the undermentioned members of the Committees at their residencies:

TOWN COMMITTEE:
Mr Edmundus Burn, High Constable, 23, North-street.
" William Catt, Junior, 80, Western-road,
" James Cordy, 53, North-street,
" Frederick Cooper, 48 Ship-street,
" William Lambert, 53, Western-road.

COMMISSIONERS' COMMITTEE:
Mr D. M. Folkard, 138, North-street,
" James Collins, 20, Ship street,
" William Barnes, 126, St. James's-street,
" Philip Walton, Norfolk Hotel,
" William Hallett, Bristol Hotel.

SOMERS CLARKE, Honorary Secretary, 8, Ship-street.

LEWIS SLIGHT, Clerk to the Commissioners.
Town Hall, 28th March, 1844.

SUBSCRIPTIONS RECEIVED SINCE OUR LAST.

	£	s			£	s
G. S. Dickins, Esq	5	0		Miss Holloway	1	0
The Old Brighton Gas Company	5	5		The Town Criers	1	0
Mr William Lambert	5	0		Mrs Seymour	1	0
Rev. H. Way, Denham	5	5		W. Borrer, jun., Esq.	1	0
Sir M J Tierney, Bart.	5	0		Mr E Butler	1	0
T S., Esq. by Messrs Boys and Bellingham	5	0		A Friend, by Mr Puget	1	0
				Mr W. P. Gorringe	1	0
Charles Cobby, Esq.	3	3		T. H. Statham, Esq.	1	0
Three Friends, by Mr Harrap	3	3		Marlow Sidney, Esq.	1	0
General St. John	3	0		Bright Smith, Esq.	1	0
A few Friends, by Mr S. Joel	1	17		Mrs Bright Smith	1	0
Folkard and Cobbett	2	2		T. B. Winter, Esq.	1	0
Thomas Atkinson, Esq.	2	2		Miss A. Holloway	1	0
Messrs. Thomas and Edward Clarke, London	2	2		Mr H. Weekes	1	0
				Mr P. Martin	1	0
Alderman Wilson	2	0		E Purner, Esq.	1	0
The Heathcoughe	2	0		Mr W. F Dadley.	1	0
Captain Greeves James.	2	0		Mrs Dadley	1	0
Mr Lawrence	2	0		Mrs Wood	1	0
A. A. Lindo, Esq., London, by Mr Woolf	2	0		Solomon Bennett, Esq., London	1	0
Madame Lefaudeux	1	10		L. L. L.	1	0
The Reporters and Compositors of the Brighton Gazette	1	10		W. Verrall, Esq.	1	0
				Major Baynton	0	10
R. T. Goodwin, Esq., N.S., Bombay	1	1		W. Penfold, Esq	0	10
				Mr W. Faithfull	0	10
Mr C. Cheesman	1	1		Mr J. Maddocks	0	10
H. M. Blaker, Esq.	1	1		Mr S. Joel	0	10
Thomas Blaker, Esq.	1	1		J. and A. Sayers	0	10
Miss Hannington	1	1		Mr C. Phillps	0	10
Miss Nightingale and young ladies	1	1		W. W. Burrell, Esq.	0	10
Rev. J. S. Wiggett	1	1		Mrs Boyle	0	10
Mr P. Walton	1	1		Captain Phillips	0	10
Mr Brewster	1	0		Mr Jon. Streeter	0	10
Mr John Ball	1	0		A Lady	0	10
Mr Silverthorne	1	0		Mr J. Bloan	0	10
Captain Martin	1	0		Lady Gould	0	10
Miss Parnell	1	0		Lady Townshend	0	10
Mr W Rigden	1	0		Mrs Frank	0	10
Mr Rous	1	0		Mr F. Wright	0	10
Mr Fowler	1	0		Mr R. Cobham	0	10
Rev. Thomas Cooke	1	0		Mr J. Blaker, sen	0	10
Countess of Athlone	1	0		Mr Erasmus Pecock	0	10
				Mr G. Langdon, jun.	0	10

TO POLICE OFFICERS.

NOTICE IS HEREBY GIVEN, that the Commissioners, acting under the Brighton Police Act, are about to appoint a person, whose age shall not be less than Twenty five years or exceeding Forty-five, to act as CHIEF OFFICER of POLICE in the Town of Brighton, at a salary of One Hundred and Fifty Pounds per annum.

Persons desirous of becoming Candidates for such appointment will send a written application, with testimonials to character and service, to me, at my Office, on or before Wednesday, the 17th day of April instant.

By order of the said Commissioners,
LEWES SLIGHT,
Town Hall,   Clerk.
Brighton, 4th April, 1844.

Above: Advertisement for the vacant post of Brighton's Chief of Police after Solomon's death.
Left: Subscription for the Solomon family.

The white hood was placed over his head and the rope around his neck. After the chaplain read the burial service, the trapdoor bolt was drawn and he fell from sight.

Lawrence was buried within the precincts of the gaol. In the following year, when the gaol was pulled down, his body was exhumed. His head was taken to the Queen's Head stables where it was placed on temporary exhibition. A charge of twopence was made for those who wished a viewing. Eventually Lawrence, along with the bodies of scores of men and women who had gone to the scaffold, was reburied in the west end of the old churchyard.

As for Solomon's large family, after a public meeting the sum of £500 was donated by the Town Commissioners, the local circus gave its night's takings and the Queen sent a sum of £50. The Brighton Jewish community, relatively small at that time, contributed a handsome 50 guineas, a sum quite out of proportion to its modest resources. In all a total of well over £1,000 was raised, the equivalent of £66,000 today. Solomon's children were offered free education.

Henry Solomon was a great Chief Police Officer and his murder, which was reported all over the country, evoked enormous sympathy. The split-personality town which he served continued its topsy-turvy career, its low-life vices as much on view as its conspicuous gaiety, its seedy crime matching its good works, its petty misdemeanours ending too often in tragedy.

7

THE ONION PIE MURDER

Gun Hill, 1851

Almost immediately after William French's death some people had their doubts. The whispering started almost straight away. Rumour fed on rumour, busying tongues, so that the events at Gun Hill were gossiped about in every quarter of the parish and beyond. In all the little communities – Holmes Hill, Muddles Green, Burgh Hill, Scrapers Hill, Whitesmith, Hale Green, Pick Hill, Chiddingly-Street – they suspected something was amiss. The 31-year-old farm labourer, they were saying, had died so unexpectedly . . . and him so healthy . . . the circumstances . . . well, the circumstances . . . they had been plain enough to see . . . his wife, people said, had been carrying on with another man . . . a younger man . . . and her the mother of a little boy, too . . . and they were known throughout the district, William and Sarah . . . and their families . . . she was a Piper . . . plenty of them round about . . . and young Hickman . . . he was from a local family . . . always visiting the Frenches . . . working for his great-uncle George Gander over at West Street Farm . . . not far from the Frenches' cottage next to Gatehouse Farm.

And all so sudden.

On 24 December 1851, William French was at his work, threshing corn in the barn at Stream Farm, Chiddingly. It was back-breaking labour that began at seven in the morning and ended at five. But at least he was in work for the winter and not existing on parish handouts, or worse, being forced into the Union workhouse at Hellingly.

French was looking forward to his supper that day. His wife had promised him an onion pie. 'A rarity' was how he described it to his workmate and near neighbour, William Funnell.

But the next day, Christmas Day, French was ill in bed. The pie, he was to say later, had 'interrupted his insides'. He remained in bed on Boxing Day, which was a holiday, and went back to work on Saturday 27 December – but returned home after only a few minutes. By the weekend he had recovered and was well enough to go with Sarah to the Zoar Chapel at Lower Dicker, a round walk of six miles or so. The following week he worked without complaint and again on the Sunday went to chapel.

75

On Monday 5 January he complained once more of stomach pains and the next two days he could not go to work. His wife was saying on the Wednesday that she thought he had improved but late in the evening, just before midnight, he had turned to her in bed and muttered his last words: 'You be my wife, bean't you?'

Despite the hour, neighbours came at once in reponse to her cries. Nimrod Willis, the doctor's assistant, was sent for and Sarah told him how her husband had suddenly died although she did say that earlier he had been vomiting and had had fainting fits and violent palpitations of the heart. Willis expressed surprise that he had not been summoned earlier but Sarah explained that her husband insisted there was no need for a doctor, that he would soon recover.

Dr Holman conducted a post-mortem on 10 January and on the same day, at the inquest at The Gun Inn, stated that death was the result of strangulation of the intestines. Mr F.H. Gell, the East Sussex Coroner, recorded death from natural causes. On the following day, William French was buried.

Sarah now felt some sense of relief. Inquests are always trying for women who have murdered their husbands.

But there was a general unease. The doubts were too great, the whispers too loud. People like William's brother, John, as well as the neighbours, must have had some doubts about what had occurred. In fact, it was John French's initial doubts that were to lead to official enquiries being made. He heard somewhere that poison had been bought.

How people talked! Sarah was for ever having to answer questions. Sometimes, too, she seems to have volunteered information. On 5 January she met Harriet Boniface, a shepherd's wife, outside Bourship Cottage at Lower Dicker and told her that her husband would not let her send for a doctor. At the same time, she said that she expected him to die.

To others, such as her neighbour Mary Bennett, Sarah was to express her anxiety about what might be found at the post-mortem. It seems that she was giving off signals all the time. And, of course, the involvement of young James Hickman was spoken about. He was a regular visitor to the Frenches and it had been noticed.

No doubt all the fifteen or so households that made up the small Gun Hill community were exchanging views. Who among them could fail to be interested? After all, they all knew the Frenches well enough. They had lived in their Gun Hill cottage for the past seven or eight years. Imagine the sensation. Chiddingly parish was not essentially different from other rural communities of the time. It would admit to the usual round of rural crime, some petty theft, poaching, breaking into barns for sacks of corn, stealing fowl and the like, for these were grim days of bleak deprivation. But this was a different matter. There had been an inquest: the poor man was buried. But people still talked. Murder was hinted at. Nothing like this had occurred before in Gun Hill. People knew each other here: they carried the histories of other families in their heads.

At the Zoar Baptist Chapel, Lower Dicker, the attendance for each Sunday service used to number 500, people coming from the surrounding hamlets and villages. And

Zoar Chapel, Little Dicker, 2005. (Alan Skinner)

now there was to unfold a shameful drama of deceit, illicit love and murder, in which two of their regular members, Sarah French and James Hickman, were to play principal roles.

Nothing could have prepared these little rural backwaters for the kind of story they were about to hear, a story involving people they knew, people who were, they might have thought, no different from themselves.

It was during the fortnight after her husband's death that Sarah moved to Popp's Farm three-quarters of a mile or so from Gatehouse Farm, occupying part of a cottage next to William Muggridge, a small farmer. She was to be at Popp's for very few days, and the reason for the move was never revealed. Did she feel the need to leave the house where she had murdered her husband? Were the neighbours now more openly doubtful of her?

One conclusion is simply that she and her lover, Hickman, wanted more discreet opportunities to meet each other. Popp's and West Street Farm, where Hickman lived and worked, were very close together. He might well have been instrumental in arranging the move: he certainly moved Sarah's furniture.

Then on 17 January, in the evening, quite unexpectedly, Simon Peter Lower, schoolmaster and Vestry member fulfilling the role of Parish Constable, called at Popp's Farm. He was to escort Sarah to The Gun Inn. Another inquest had been convened.

'I suppose you have heard the rumours?' he asked her.

'You mean about my husband?'

Of course she had heard the rumours. Who had not? Lower, along with Super-intendent Flanagan and Inspector Dawes of the East Sussex Police, had been making enquiries in recent weeks.

There is no record of what passed at this evening inquest at The Gun Inn. Sarah was kept there overnight, returning home the following day.

Two days later, in the morning, Superintendent Flanagan again went to Popp's. He put a series of questions to Sarah. She told him that her husband was 'taken bad in his bowels on Sunday morning and on Monday he was a little better and thought he should go to work. On Tuesday he was also better and on Wednesday night he died.'

She told the Superintendent that she had given him a diet of flour gruel. On the Wednesday evening she had given him threepennyworth of brandy which Hickman had brought from The Gun Inn, but he had been unable to keep that down. She also mentioned that in November and December her husband had bought indigo-coloured arsenic from Noakes's shop in Chiddingly. This was true: the house was infested with mice. Lard sprinkled with arsenic was their solution to this problem. And some bills, she told the Superintendent, were due to be paid and these were worrying her husband. Over Christmas he had been in low spirits over them. He had cried at the very thought of them.

Or did he cry at the thought of his obviously crumbling marriage? He had complained to Hickman's father about the young man's over-frequent visits. Again, of course, the tears could be put down to his generally debilitated state: he had after all had onion pie on Christmas Eve.

No, Sarah said in answer to that question which seemed to dog her, she had not sent for a doctor.

The Superintendent then put to her the same question as had Lower. Had she heard the rumours? She agreed she had, answering that if her husband had taken poison he must have taken it himself. This hint at the possibility of suicide was never again raised.

At this point, Flanagan took her in a cart to The Six Bells at Chiddingly, where the second inquest was resumed. Her husband's body had been exhumed. Dr Holman had carried out a second post-mortem and the body of William French now lay in the belfry of Chiddingly Church.

This second inquest was once more adjourned, but this time Sarah was taken into custody and lodged in Lewes Gaol. James Hickman was also placed in custody, although there was no evidence offered that he had played any part in what was suspected as a murder, nor was he ever charged with any offence.

The reason for the postponement was that Dr Holman, having conducted a more detailed examination of the stomach and contents, now suspected the presence of arsenic in the body. Then, safeguarding his reputation, he stated that 'if no poison had been found, I should certainly believe the death to have arisen from that cause [strangulation of the intestine] alone'.

The whole of the stomach and intestines were sent for analysis by Professor Taylor at Guy's Hospital. The inquest at The Six Bells was reconvened on 2 February when

A 2005 view of the Six Bells at Chiddingly, where the inquest into William French's death was held. (Alan Skinner)

the professor presented his findings. Up to eleven grains of arsenic had been administered, he said. Three or four were enough to kill a man. In his view French might have been given it in several small doses, but the professor was confident that one large dose had been administered in the twenty-four hours before death.

A variety of witnesses now appeared before the Coroner – doctors, neighbours, shopkeepers. John French, who also worked at Stream Farm, had last seen his brother on Christmas Eve. 'He was then in good health,' he told the Court. William was 'an able-bodied man'. Tabitha Pelling, the dressmaker, who lived in a cottage adjoining the Frenches, swore that three days before his death 'he looked as usual', and Mary Funnell, another near neighbour, was later to assure the Court that French was 'not a very ailing man'. When she had seen the corpse, shortly after death, she noticed, 'the lips appeared to be sore and were covered with little red spots'. Her husband William knew the dead man as 'a very strong man' in good health. 'I never heard the deceased complain of illness,' he declared, 'until after he had eaten the onion pie.'

Among the most powerful statements were those of William Funnell and Henry Hickman, father of James.

Funnell told the court: 'About Christmas he [French] told me that young Hickman was always at his house and he had spoken to his [Hickman's] father about it. He appeared to be uneasy in his mind, but did not say why he was so. He was a very quiet man and not much given to talking.'

Later, Henry Hickman told the court:

I had a conversation with the deceased on the Sunday week before he died. I met him coming from Chapel; he was alone; it was towards one o'clock. He overtook me and I said, 'Well, Mr. French, how be you?' He replied, 'Not very well.' I asked him who that was before us. He said, 'It is my wife and your Jim' and he said, 'I don't very well like it.' I said, 'No more do I.' He said then, 'I wish you would tell him to keep away from my house.' I asked if he ever saw any underhand dealings between my son and his wife. He said, 'No.' I said, 'He tells me you asked him to come and read a book to the little boy who was ill.' He said, 'I did.' I asked him why he did not tell him to keep away if he did not like it. He said the reason why he did not tell him to do so was, if he spoke to his wife she would say he was jealous of her and he thought she would make away with herself.

The following Sunday I saw the deceased going to Chapel with his wife arm-in-arm . . . I told my son what Mr. French had said, and he replied, if Mr. French had told him he did not want him to come he would not have gone. I have frequently told him not to go there. He said French had asked him to go and read to his little boy who was ill.

After this, James Hickman admitted that he and Mrs French sometimes kissed, and that she sometimes sat on his knee, that they had talked of marriage, that he had been at the house on the night that French ate the onion pie. Hickman was also to say that he heard the sick man upstairs, retching and vomiting violently on the night of Tuesday, 6 January. He had drunk nearly a kettle of water, Sarah told Hickman, who had then suggested a doctor be sent for. Sarah, he said, rejected the idea. Her husband had refused to have a doctor. Instead, Hickman went up to The Gun Inn for brandy.

What finally persuaded the inquest jury that Sarah French had a case to answer was the evidence of Mrs Naomi Crowhurst, the wife of the Lower Horsebridge veterinary surgeon. She identified Sarah as the woman who bought about two teaspoonfuls of arsenic from her two days before William French's death. It was certainly Mrs Crowhurst's evidence that Sarah most feared. 'They will take me and hang me,' she told Mary Bennett after the inquest, 'because Mrs. Crowhurst swears I am the woman who bought the poison of her.'

At the end of the day, the inquest jury returned a verdict of Wilful Murder against Sarah French. The Coroner committed her for trial at the Sussex Spring Assizes, held at Lewes.

The case before Mr Baron Parke lasted two days – 19 and 20 March 1852. It aroused considerable interest and was reported extensively in local newspapers and *The Times*.

During her time awaiting trial Sarah was seriously ill, so that when she appeared in front of the judge she presented a forlorn figure. 'The prisoner was paralysed and would require to be seated . . . She appeared greatly changed since her committal, having lost all her colour.' She was never to recover her health.

In the waiting period, on 19 February, Sarah had made an unexpected and dramatic statement about James Hickman. In this she said that he had confessed to her that on two occasions he had administered poison to her husband – once in the onion pie, once in his gruel; another time, when she was complaining about French being out late at night, she said that Hickman had told her he would give him something that would make him stay out later. Sarah also claimed that Hickman had shown her a package of arsenic. If she told anyone of what he had said, he had threatened to leave her. These allegations were read to the Court early in the proceedings.

There were two main strands to the case. The first concerned the poison, how and where it was purchased and by whom. The second related to Sarah's liaison with Hickman and whether he had played any part in the murder. He had not, of course, been charged with any offence and merely appeared as a witness. Nevertheless, he had been kept in custody during this pre-trial period.

In the two weeks before French's death, there was certainly arsenic in the cottage. James Noakes, the grocer in Chiddingly-Street, explained that he had sold William French a halfpennyworth of arsenic on both 1 November and 20 December. French had told him they had an infestation of mice. When French returned home on the second occasion he asked his wife to hide the arsenic for fear their six-year-old son found it. Sarah had put the poison in a cupboard in the small brewhouse in the garden. James Hickman was present when French arrived with the arsenic, which some might have considered significant. It was only days after this, on Christmas Day, that French was very ill after eating the onion pie.

It was, however, Sarah's purchase of arsenic which concerned both the inquest and the Assize Court. Evidence was brought that she had purchased the poison on 5 January. Had the half ounce that French had brought home only a fortnight earlier been used up?

Unlike her husband, Sarah did not go to Noakes, where she was known. Instead she walked to Horsebridge. She failed to buy arsenic at Deadman's, the grocery and drapery shop. She was again unsuccessful at Uriah Clarke's. The latter told the Court that he had known Sarah for eight years. Nevertheless, she denied having been in his shop. She now made her way to the veterinary surgeon's shop.

Here, the vet's wife, 28-year-old Naomi Crowhurst, reluctantly sold Sarah twopennyworth of white arsenic. Mrs Crowhurst asked this woman, a stranger to her, why she wanted arsenic. Learning that it was for mice, Mrs Crowhurst warned her of its dangers, writing 'Poison' on the bottle.

Sarah denied at both inquest and trial ever having been in Crowhurst's shop and much time was taken up over the matter of identification. Her bonnet and shawl were produced. At the inquest she had been asked to change from her widow's weeds so that Mrs Crowhurst could be more certain that this was the woman who had come to the shop.

Other witnesses were called to say that they had seen Sarah on the Horsebridge road that day. She conceded that she had gone there to buy ribbons. Perhaps she had. But she was also the woman who had bought twopennyworth of arsenic from Mrs Crowhurst.

Asked why she had not called a doctor to her husband, Sarah constantly maintained that French refused to have one. There is evidence, however, and it is strange that nothing more was made of this, that Willis, Dr Holman's assistant, had given French some pills for nausea and headaches just before Christmas. How does this tie in with a man refusing to have a doctor? And further, does it suggest that some attempt had been made to poison him some time before Christmas Eve? There was poison in the house from 20 December. Indeed, there might have been some left over from the purchase made by French on 1 November when he first brought home the indigo-coloured arsenic from Noakes's shop. But nothing came up at either inquest or trial on either of these matters.

After Sarah's statement accusing him of the murder, James Hickman becomes a figure of even greater interest at the trial than he had been at the inquest. He is described in *The Times* as having 'the appearance of a labouring man', which does not take us very far. The *Sussex Express*, however, makes us see him anew. He is not as we might have imagined. 'He is about 18 years of age but scarcely looks as old as that.' Here then is this boyish figure, really a twenty-year-old, who might have been French's poisoner.

Hickman had first come to know the Frenches well in the last year. It is assumed that they were all, previously, as chapel-goers and as people living in the same area, on nodding acquaintance. At that time Hickman had been courting Sarah's sister, Jane Piper, then aged about seventeen. In the spring of 1851, when Jane came to stay at the Frenches' cottage, Hickman visited her there. Much was made at the trial about when this relationship foundered and that with Sarah started up. Possibly there was a period when Hickman was setting his cap at both ladies. This was certainly the view of one juror.

Hickman: She asked me if I would marry her if her husband was dead and I said yes.
A juror: What, and courting her sister at the same time?
Hickman: Her sister had got another sweetheart then.

According to Hickman, he and Jane Piper stopped seeing each other about six weeks before Christmas. But his regular visits to the cottage began in the autumn when he was invited by William French to read to his sick son. Exactly when the affair between Sarah and Hickman started is not clear. Perhaps it is reasonable to date it from November 1851, making it a romance of a very short duration.

On both of his appearances, before the coroner and the judge, Hickman was at pains to imply that Sarah took all the initiatives.

'She asked me if I liked her as well as I did her sister. I said "No" and she said, "Why not?" I then said, "Because you are married." She then asked me if I should like her if she was not married and I told her I liked her very well. This was about a month before Christmas.'

Hickman had taken to visiting the cottage two or three times a week, spending an hour or so there. Sometimes Sarah had turned up at West Street Farm asking him to visit. On occasion he seems to have gone out for a drink with French, although it is apparent from the evidence of William Funnell and Henry Hickman that there must have been a cooling-off in the friendship of the two men. Often Hickman read to little James French.

About those times when she kissed him or when she sat on his knee, the young man was quick to say that he did not always respond. He was, of course, anxious now to distance himself from Sarah, who had tried to blame him for her husband's death. He must by now have realised that it was she who had poisoned her husband. Asked if she ever 'made free with him' in her husband's absence, he replied that 'She never pulled me about improperly.' It ought to be said here that sexual intercourse did not take place before William French's death.

Still, there seems to have been much talk about love. Hickman was given a ring by Sarah to keep in remembrance of her and this was produced in court. There were references, too, to future marriage. What would he do, Sarah had asked him, if her husband died?

'I told her I did not know. I did not mind much about it.'

The question presents a few difficulties. What of the response? Was he really so off-hand? Or was he simply trying to impress upon the court that it was Sarah who always made the advances?

But did he not wonder about such questions? Ought she to be posing them, asking about what might happen if French were to die? Sarah appears to have convinced Hickman that French had not long to live, that there was something wrong with her husband's stomach. It may be for this reason that Hickman was not so surprised as he might have been when French did die.

Immediately after French's death Hickman was being pursued as a prospective bridegroom. Even on the night of French's burial, Sarah was asking him to marry her. They had better wait a twelvemonth, he had told her. It would look better. Sarah, however, was afraid that in that time she would lose him.

On the night of the funeral, for the first time, she and Hickman shared a bed. Is there a degree of callousness here on the part of both of them? What are the objections? Intercourse? Intercourse so soon after the death? Intercourse so soon after the death in French's bed?

On the other hand, we should accept that this was the first occasion that sexual intercourse had occurred. Had there been no opportunities? Or had there been, in spite of all else, some inhibitions, a reluctance to commit adultery? Had their conduct been to some degree regulated by their chapel teaching?

What disturbed the court greatly was to learn that on this night, when Hickman and Sarah came together as lovers for the first time, their bed was shared by Jane Piper and that little James French's bed was in the same room. There is no indication, by the way, that intercourse took place while Jane was in the bed.

One explanation for the bed-sharing on 11 January – and there was a bed in the kitchen in addition to that upstairs – may be that on this night of emotions, highly charged after the recent events, Sarah needed the comfort not just of James Hickman but also of her younger sister. Sarah French, guilty of murder, still anxious perhaps about rumours, feeling even now only partially safe after her husband's burial, was no doubt a confused woman, seeking solace from the two people she most certainly loved.

During the next few days, the lovers slept together on several occasions, first at the cottage in Gun Hill and later at Popp's Farm. Where did they think it was all leading to?

At the conclusion of the two-day trial, Mr Rodwell, who, at the direction of the judge, had looked after Sarah's interests in court, addressed the jury. He suggested that there was no proof of Sarah's having poisoned her husband. It could have been Hickman, whom Sarah had accused in her statement before the trial began. Rodwell argued that Hickman might have been after a share of a legacy of £500 – today valued at £35,000 – which apparently was coming to Sarah. She had told Hickman that she would keep him, that he would never need to work again. Indeed it was a considerable sum, though whether it existed, and whether Hickman believed in its existence, is not known. The issue of the legacy is tantalising but it seems to have been introduced fleetingly into the case against Hickman and then dropped. Rodwell did not, could not, accuse Hickman of murder. He simply placed seeds of uncertainty in the minds of the jury, arguing that Sarah was entitled to the benefit of the doubt.

It took the jury an hour and three-quarters to reach a conclusion. Finally they returned a verdict of guilty, although the Foreman made the judge aware that some of the jurymen believed her to be more an accessory before the fact rather than the principal agent. Mr Rodwell had certainly argued her case persuasively.

But it was enough for the judge. Even if she had not put the poison in her husband's food, he declared that if she knew of someone else who was carrying out such a crime she was guilty of Wilful Murder. She was sentenced to death.

Sarah French, four foot ten in height, was described for the first time in *The Times* on the day the verdict was announced.

'The prisoner, although stated in the calendar to be only 27 years old, bears all the appearance of a woman of 40 and her countenance is one of the most repulsive character.'

But then perhaps *The Times* believed that criminals of the lower classes ought to look repulsive, that their vices, their criminality, ought to be etched in their faces. As it is we have no reliable description of Sarah French save that she was a tiny woman.

Lewes Gaol. (Courtesy of Lewes Reference Library)

She was ill after being taken in custody and remained so for the few remaining days of her life.

'It appears that she has been subject to fits,' *The Times* continued, 'and since she has been in gaol she has become partially paralysed, and it was consequently necessary to have her lifted into the Court by two turnkeys; and she was placed on a chair in front of the dock, where she sat apparently in a kind of stupor during the whole of the trial, not betraying the least emotion.'

As for James Hickman, the press emphasised his lack of emotion too. He made no kind of response when he heard 'his wretched paramour's fate'. Yet how should he react? Should he appear to approve the sentence? Or distressed as though he too were guilty? Certainly by now he must have fallen out of love with Sarah in view of her having tried to implicate him. But how do twenty-year-old country boys know what expressions they ought to show in front of the full and fearsome majesty of the law?

Hickman's statements in court do sometimes conflict. Did he or did he not agree to marry Sarah if her husband were to die? Was he or was he not surprised at French's death? Did he never suspect anything? As far as he knew, he said, French had 'something bad the matter with him and the doctors could not do him any good'. Sarah had told him this and he had believed her. She had said to him that her husband 'was frequently taken very bad in his inside at night and that it would kill him'. It seems that he never doubted her.

The truth of it seems to be that an immature boy, flattered by an older woman, became involved in matters too complex for him to appreciate. He was thoughtless of the consequences of his liaison; he was selfish, scornful perhaps of poor, wretched William French; he was feckless, ignoring his father's advice. But that does not make him a murderer. In any event, on the day before her execution, Sarah confessed to the Chaplain that she alone had poisoned her husband, that Hickman had had no part in it and that she had implicated him solely with the idea of 'making matters lighter with herself'. But had not Hickman, at a time of so many rumours of which he must have been aware, never paused to wonder what had happened? Had he no suspicions? It may, of course, be difficult to think such thoughts about a lover. Perhaps Hickman really did discount the rumours. Perhaps until the last days of January he really did believe that William French had died of a strangulation of the intestines.

And Sarah, what of her? She turns out in the end to be a pathetic, prematurely aged figure, ill, paralysed, not very attractive to look at, not the sultry temptress we might have imagined. Several witnesses attested to the fact that she and her husband

Sarah French's death certificate. (Crown Copyright. Reproduced with the permission of the Controller of HMSO)

seemed happily married. But then passion sometimes gets in the way and disrupts lives. What robs us of some greater understanding and compassion for Sarah French is not her love affair but the manner in which she disposed of her husband. It is not solely the murder which nauseates but the callousness, the cold-bloodedness, the watching him die over a period of a fortnight, feeding him poison over several days. This is what ultimately takes our sympathy from her.

Sarah French hanged at Lewes Gaol on 10 April 1852. A crowd of three or four thousand, some of them arriving from distant parts by train, assembled in North Street and Little East Street. The windows of all neighbouring houses facing the prison were filled with spectators. They saw her frail figure carried to the scaffold, saw her supported there over the trapdoor, saw her struggles which lasted some minutes as she choked at the rope's end. Her body was finally taken from the scaffold and placed in a lead coffin and buried within the outer walls of the prison.

James Hickman returned to West Street Farm. Later he married, had a family, lived in a cottage in Gun Hill and continued working as a farm labourer.

The Onion Pie Murder, as it is sometimes called, touched a whole close-knit world, stained some lives. Even the great world beyond heard of it, read about it. It was a cruel murder committed by a very ordinary woman who, until the last turbulent months of her life, had the reputation of being a loving wife and a caring mother and a good neighbour.

Perhaps it is possible to judge Sarah French too harshly. Was she simply an uneducated peasant woman of crude sensibilities, caught up in a whirl of emotions which were beyond control, who in the space of a few months was cast in the role of a major character in a minor, sordid, rural tragedy? Was she no more than a sad, obsessed, misguided woman betrayed by her passions? That would seem to be the best analysis.

8

THE ENYS ROAD MURDERS

Eastbourne, 1912

Perhaps at the time it seemed that, though desperately tragic in its outcome, this was an uncomplicated case. At least, it was as far as the police could tell. It was obvious that a murder of the most atrocious kind had been committed, that the house had been set on fire, and that the murderer had then committed suicide. There were of course problems of identity, as the dead were not local people. According to neighbours they were renting the house for a few weeks. Even so, such matters were normally easily resolved by the police.

But the horrific murder at Eastbourne in the quiet and fashionable district of Upperton was a jigsaw puzzle. It remains so. So many pieces just do not fit, so many others are missing. Over the next few weeks the story unravelled, though never completely, so that even today answers to questions about this absorbing mystery are outstanding. Even the principal witnesses, those closest to the victims, had never divined the mystery which was at the centre of the Enys Road affair. They were just as surprised as total strangers at some of the revelations.

Florence Paler first met Robert Hicks Murray in 1907. After some time Murray asked the tall, slim, auburn-haired girl to live with him. They would get married, he said. They found and furnished a house in Marjorie Grove, Clapham Common, and went to live there. But they did not marry and Florence, who in the next two years had two children by Murray, was naturally anxious about their position. And her mother and other relatives who disapproved of the irregular liaison refused to maintain contact with her.

In spite of the rift with her family, Florence and Murray were very happy, for the most part. He was usually kind to her and they were never short of money. They lived a pleasant life in Marjorie Grove. He rose early, helped around the house, strolled on the Common in the morning, went to afternoon cricket matches and came home for tea. He used to take Florence to the theatre in their early days together, sitting in the stalls and dress circle, though more recently in the less expensive upper circle or pit. As a captain in the Gordon Highlanders, Murray was frequently absent on military duties.

Florence never met any members of Murray's family. He told her that his late father had been a barrister in Watford, as was his brother. His sister, he said, was married to

Captain Hunter of the Royal Irish Guards. But generally Murray declined to talk about his family and on at least one occasion, when she was asking questions, he had threatened to kill her and the children. 'I will make a clean sweep of us all,' he threatened. On another occasion he said to her, 'I will tell you my history some day and it will astonish you.' Was there some awful deed in the past? 'I always had at the back of my mind,' Florence said, 'a feeling that some day something terrible would happen.'

Sometimes she had queried why he never had an army uniform or a military dress-sword in the house. No army papers were ever delivered there and this puzzled her. But whenever she raised queries, he would ask her, 'Aren't you satisfied? You get all you want. Then why bother?' Or he might be even more menacing. 'You interfere in my affairs and I will kill you.'

It must have caused some anxieties that Murray was constantly so evasive. It does seem rather odd. How is it that a woman normally knows her husband's profession? Does she have to discover it by ferreting in his pockets? Does she never meet work friends and colleagues?

Florence accepted that the demands of military life required her husband to spend time away from home. But there was an occasion when she asked him where he would be during his absence. 'He gave the names of several barracks where he said he had to take duty,' she said. 'From that time he spent one day and one night with me and one day and one night elsewhere. He also began to return home late at night. Previously he had been a total abstainer but now he commenced to drink.'

In the summer of July 1911 Florence and Murray spent five weeks in Herne Bay, taking a house in the name of Morris. Now isn't this curious? How did Murray ever explain the reason why he chose to use a false name? And how was it that Florence did not enquire more deeply? Few wives would be so acquiescent. While at Herne Bay he went off for two or three weeks, leaving her with the children: he had charge of troops called out in connection with a railway strike, he told her.

In the summer of 1912, Murray was again absent on army duties, but he picked up Florence and the children on 15 July and they all went to Eastbourne for a long holiday. They had put their furniture into storage, Florence believing that on their return to London they were going to move into a larger house. Murray told her he could not stay in Eastbourne longer than one night because he had to return to duty in Kingston upon Thames. This of course echoed events of the previous year at Herne Bay. The next day, 16 July, answering the call of duty, he left, though he did come back to Eastbourne twice a week.

This time they were masquerading under the name of Stirling. But she apparently asked no questions about this. She was sure it had nothing to do with money. Her husband always appeared to have plenty. Some quirk, she probably told herself. She played along with it, perhaps afraid not to.

At Eastbourne, Florence stayed in dismal rooms at the Annington Road house of Police Sergeant Robert Packham. She was pregnant again and fretting for the return to London. She stayed there until Monday 12 August, when she moved into a bed-sitting room at 31 Whitley Road, staying there until Saturday 17 August.

Mr and Mrs Meads at the Whitley Road lodgings also knew the family as Stirling. Florence told Mrs Meads that her husband was a soldier. Not that Mr Meads, an old soldier, was impressed by Murray. In his view, he was not at all like a military man. To him, he was more like a smartly dressed clerk, which smacks of a certain perceptive class awareness. Florence also talked about their home in Clapham, but apparently did not mention that they hoped to be moving. According to Mrs Meads, the Stirlings were affectionate towards one another. She seemed more impressed with Florence than her husband was with Murray, remarking on her clothes and jewellery.

The landlady recalled that Murray arranged to come and fetch the family at about ten o'clock on Saturday morning, 17 August. He arrived at the house at about eleven o'clock and said to his wife that he had to go straight away to Seaford. Military matters as usual. He arranged to come back at seven in the evening.

But he did not arrive until ten o'clock at night. Once more he excused himself, claiming that he now had to see some soldiers off on some late duty or other. He gave Florence £23 to buy the children some clothes.

Murray finally arrived on the Sunday afternoon. They went to town, walked along the seafront, had tea. Finally they went to the station but then Murray announced quite out of the blue, 'We won't go home tonight. I have a furnished house down here lent me by Captain Mackie, a friend of mind in the regiment. We will go there.'

This was a sudden decision and naturally Florence was profoundly disappointed. She had spent several unhappy weeks in Eastbourne. 'No one knows how unhappy I was in those apartments in Eastbourne,' she was to say, 'wondering and wondering what was going to happen, as I felt sure that something was going to take place.' What was it that had so concerned her? She does not indicate anywhere the cause of these fears. Undoubtedly, being alone in a strange town with only the children, and seeing her husband only twice a week, she was lonely. But frightened? At the station, when Murray announced the change of plan, she had pleaded with him to take them all back to London. She was so frightened, she told him.

But he had laughed away her fears, telling her that they would be all right because it was a fine house, bigger and better than any she had ever lived in. After leaving the luggage at the station, they went quite late at night to Enys Road, stopping only at a garage where Murray bought a can of petrol. It was for his friend Mackie who had a motor car, he told her.

When for the first time Florence saw the house, brick-built, foursquare, solid, she was even more anxious. To her, late at night, it looked 'so old, so dark, so big, and so lonely'.

Inside, the house was in some disorder, the kitchen grate full of charred papers and, in the sink, unwashed crockery and cutlery. There was a perambulator in the kitchen and Florence asked him about it. It belonged to Captain Mackie's child, he said. Murray seemed irritable with his son, which was unusual. He was nervous about something, his hands shaking all the time at supper.

Afterwards Murray showed her round the house. 'We can go everywhere in the house except that room,' he said, indicating one of the first floor bedrooms. 'They have locked up their silver in there.'

For the rest of the Sunday night, Florence was worried. Something was wrong.

The following morning, James Pocock, a turnkey with the East-bourne Water Company, raised the alarm. He was just starting work when, at about six o'clock, he heard what he thought were gun-shots, eight reports in all, three followed by a pause and then three more and after another pause, two more. He ran to the corner of Enys Road and saw smoke coming from the upstairs window of one of the houses, number 14. At the front

No. 14 Enys Road, Eastbourne, as it is today. (Alan Skinner)

of the house there was a woman in bloodstained night clothes. She was standing on the short flight of steps, screaming hysterically. A man had shot her children, she was shouting, he had killed them, and then she turned and ran back into the house. Pocock found a house with a telephone and called the police and the fire brigade.

Alice Farrant, a housemaid at 47 Enys Road, heard the shots and saw the smoke issuing from the windows of the house opposite. She thought the woman on the steps was shouting 'He has shot me!' and certainly she was bleeding from a neck wound. Alice was not deterred. She ran across the road and into the house and made her way upstairs but made little further progress because of the density of the smoke from one of the rooms. At this point PC Thomas Harding arrived. He asked Alice to go downstairs to look after the injured woman. She went back down and bathed the distressed woman's neck. Shortly after this, Alice and the Revd W.P. Jay took her, wrapped in blankets, to the vicarage.

PC Harding, a tablecloth draped over his head, tried to make his way into the room but was beaten back by the ferocity of the blaze. He was joined by William Elphick, the caretaker from number 51. He had heard the piercing screams. 'They were perfectly awful in their loudness,' Elphick said later. 'I don't think I ever heard such screams before.'

The police and fire brigade, with their horse-drawn tenders, were on the scene very quickly. The smoke and flames had not spread beyond the first-floor bedroom but the door into the passageway had been blown outwards by an explosion, and now flames were billowing out on to the landing and threatening the floor above. The firemen concentrated their efforts on the bedroom. They saved the house from being gutted, but the bedroom was burnt out and then, as the smoke cleared, the charred remains of five human bodies, practically beyond recognition, were found. There was a man, a woman and three very young children. The woman had been fully dressed except for her shoes, and the man, his body at the side of the bed and sprawled partly across the woman, had worn only a shirt. In his right hand was a revolver, containing five spent cartridges. Blood from a gunshot wound was still oozing from the man's mouth.

In this devastated bedroom were the remains of a single three-foot bed, a chest of drawers, a dressing table and a perambulator. There was a trunk too, in which a gold watch and a bracelet were found.

Once the fire had been extinguished Chief Inspector Charles Miles and Inspector Taylor, in charge of a small body of police, took possession of the house. Neither of the other two first-floor bedrooms was affected by fire. In one of these rooms Chief Inspector Miles found that a pillow and the bottom sheet on one of the two beds was saturated with blood. There were three bullet holes in the sheet and three bullets lodged in the mattress. On the floor were several cartridges and spent cases and in the chest of drawers there were twenty-eight live cartridges. Blood and brains spattered the bed, the floor and the walls. Some of the victims, perhaps all of them, had died here and not in the room in which they were found. There were empty petrol cans in this bedroom, as well as on the landing.

On the landing a few items of children's clothing were scattered. Here too were more cartridges, live and spent.

In their search police found £32 in gold, ten shillings in silver and a few copper coins. In the drawing room, on top of the piano, they found two pages torn from *Hymns Ancient and Modern*. On one page was a hymn.

> Weary of earth and laden with my sin
> I look to heaven and long to enter in;
> But there no evil thing may find a home,
> And yet I hear a voice that bids me 'Come.'
> So vile I am, how dare I hope to stand
> In the pure glory of the Holy Land,
> Before the whiteness of that throne appear?
> Yet there are hands stretched out to draw me near.

Had the murderer torn the leaves from the hymn book and left them on top of the piano, an indication of his last thoughts?

There was also a note which read: 'Am absolutely ruined and have killed all dependent on me. Should like them to bury all in one grave. God forgive me.'

Later the bodies were conveyed in coffins to the mortuary at the Town Hall, the three children placed in one coffin.

A simple heart-rending case. A tragedy. Only in the days that followed would a story of startling complexity unravel.

The injured woman seen screaming outside the house was sent on to the Princess Alice Hospital with two bullets lodged near the jugular vein, but her life was not threatened by her injuries. She identified herself as Florence Murray née Paler.

She had already given some information to Dr Adams when she was being treated at St Anne's vicarage. Despite her injuries, she was able to speak. She said that she had been shot while she was in bed 'by the Captain – Captain Hicks Murray'. She told the doctor that she had two children, a boy nearly four and a little girl. At that point, puzzled, Dr Adams returned to Enys Road. He went again to the front room and checked the bodies. There were five. Florence was mystified. They had arrived there late the previous evening, she told the doctor. There was only Captain Hicks Murray, herself and her two children there.

The Eastbourne tragedy, as illustrated in the News of the World. *Edith is on the left, and Florence with her children (and an unidentified woman) on the right.*

Who was the other woman whose body now lay in the mortuary? Who was the third child?

A telegram was sent to one of Florence's sisters living in Wimbledon. 'Come at once. In trouble – Florence.' But unable to travel to Eastbourne, this sister, whose name was not revealed, later made a reluctant statement at Wimbledon police station. She knew little enough of her sister's affairs, she said. As a result of Florence's liaison with Murray, there had been a family rift. The Palers did not care for Florence demeaning herself by cohabiting with a man, no matter how respectable he was. This anonymous sister was not even aware that he was an army captain. 'When I saw him he was in civilian clothes,' she explained. 'I only met him once. I had no idea that they were at Eastbourne until this morning.'

She knew very little about Murray but she did say: 'I understood he had always been a black sheep. His mother lives somewhere near Regents Park and I know at one time he had plenty of money for he was keeping two households going. During a portion of the time since 1910 he has been maintaining a household with my sister Florence at Marjorie Grove in Clapham Common and he has also had an establishment somewhere with my sister Edith. Where that was, I never heard.'

Mrs Beattie Vicary, another sister, did go to Eastbourne. She feared that the dead woman might prove to be her sister Edith. She came down from London late on the Monday afternoon and identified the bodies as Robert Hicks Murray, thirty-two years old; her 26-year-old sister, Edith Matilda Murray; Edith's baby, Josephine, a child aged about one year; and Florence's children, Stanley Murray aged three and Winifred Frances Murray aged two.

And now the plot thickened!

Mrs Vicary had thought that Murray was 'a man of independent means', an officer in the Scots Greys – Florence had spoken of the Gordon Highlanders – and that he had also been connected with the Territorial Army. She admitted that on occasion his mental condition had caused alarm and had worried his family. He was said to have threatened Florence, saying something to the effect, 'I will not make a disgrace of my family. I will make an end of you all.'

Matters were even less clear when the police sent a telegram to Captain Hunter of the Royal Irish Guards. Captain Hunter, they understood, was married to Murray's sister. But Chief Inspector Miles's telegram to the Captain was returned, 'Name unknown.' When Miles finally tracked down Captain Hunter they had a brief telephone conversation. 'Captain Hunter told me', the Chief Inspector said, 'that he had no knowledge of the Murrays at all. He gave me the name of his own wife – Sir Somebody's daughter.'

A neighbour in Marjorie Grove said that Murray, who was always stylishly dressed – though never, incidentally, in uniform – was rather reserved. He had heard that he had served in South Africa, had been stationed at Kingston barracks and was recently transferred to Aldershot. He spoke most warmly of Murray whom he described as having a pronounced Scottish accent.

A mystery man, then. It may be best therefore to describe first of all Florence

Murray's relationship with him up to the events in the house in Enys Road early on Monday 19 August. These details come for the most part from Florence's testimony, delivered 'in almost heroic style' at the second session of the inquest.

Florence had set up house with Murray at Marjorie Grove and in spite of the mysteries which seemed to clothe his affairs, they were happy, with two children. Then, suddenly, on to the scene came her sister Edith. Until then, for some time they had not had any contact in view of Florence's irregular liaison with Murray.

In June 1910, Edith had come to Marjorie Grove unannounced. If Florence was pleased to see her sister to begin with, as the visit went on she became increasingly disturbed at the way in which Edith and Murray behaved. After all, as far as Florence knew, this was their first meeting 'but I saw in a moment what had happened. They were instantly attracted to one another. All the evening I was in agony and neither of them spared my feelings in the least. She knew I was not married to him, though from the commencement I had been wearing a wedding ring which he gave me.'

When she was leaving Edith had said to her sister, 'What a nice man he is. I like him very much.'

And he had said to Florence, 'I think your sister Edith is the nicest woman I have ever met.'

The marriage certificate of Robert Hicks Murray and Edith Paler. Note that Robert describes himself as being of independent means. (Crown Copyright. Reproduced with the permission of the Controller of HMSO)

Was this really the first time Murray and Edith met? Or had they already met by arrangement? Were they already lovers? Were Edith and Murray playing some cruel and dangerous game with Florence?

Whatever the case, Florence never suspected that Edith and Murray would ever meet again. But she had some concerns about him. One day she discovered a receipt for an engagement ring in his pockets, which she seems to have inspected with some regularity. There is no record of how this discovery was dealt with. Did she challenge him? Did the persuasive Robert Hicks Murray have an answer for her? Or did she not dare to ask?

Several months later came the bombshell. Beattie Vicary, who had maintained contact with Florence, came to the house and told her what she had chanced upon in a church magazine – the announcement of the marriage of Murray and Edith. They had married in secret in Battersea on 26 September 1910.

After Beattie's visit, Florence had charged Murray with secretly marrying her sister. The evidence of the church magazine was too powerful and he had admitted the truth of the matter that he and Edith were legally married. He told her 'in brutal terms' that he liked Edith but said it would make no difference to Florence. They would still continue their loving association. After all, they had two children. But Florence wanted to be married too. She had the prior claim on Murray, hadn't she?

Their mother's funeral in September 1910 was the last occasion when Mrs Vicary and Florence saw Edith. Later Florence had tried to find out from Murray where Edith was but he denied knowing where she was, saying that he had given up links with her.

Florence and Murray spent Christmas 1911 at Marjorie Grove, 'the children and I enjoying ourselves in the usual Christmas fashion. But I was miserable that I was not married to him. A few days later I told him. He was very kind and appeared to understand. He suggested a Scottish marriage.' Scottish law permitted cohabiting couples to proclaim in the presence of two witnesses that they were married. For a time this suggestion satisfied Florence: only later did she realise that such an arrangement was not valid in England. And did she never consider that even if it were valid, she and Murray would be bigamists?

Before and after this occasion, Murray seems to have juggled with wonderful skill his irregular associations with the sisters. Such a frayed arrangement was bound to lead to domestic discord. Sometimes Florence threatened to leave Murray but he persuaded her to remain. On another occasion she ordered him to leave the house but he pleaded with her and promised that he would never see Edith again as he loved Florence most. She agreed to let him stay, but she must have had constant doubts.

Were there similar disagreements in the arrangement with Edith? One wonders if it was worth all of the trouble to Murray.

In Eastbourne, the policemen working on the murders gradually picked up more of the story as it had been played out locally in recent weeks.

There certainly was a Captain Mackie, just as Murray had told Florence. And Captain Mackie had taken up residence at Enys Road with his wife and child some weeks earlier. Comparison with the handwriting on the confession found in the house and the documents signed in connection with its renting proved that Robert Hicks Murray and Charles Richard Mackie were one and the same man.

From Mr Ward, house agent, there is a good description of Captain Mackie, though it may be more convenient for us to continue to think of him as Murray and to use this name. Ward described Murray as being about five foot three or four inches tall with a round face, dark hair, and a very pleasant and gentlemanly manner. He was well dressed in a grey tweed suit and white straw hat with black band. Ward noticed that two of his teeth had been stopped with gold. He was, in Ward's opinion, 'not at all military in his bearing'. Ward thought he might be an American or at least a man who had spent some time there. Murray explained that he was expecting his wife to join him but there were problems. 'He told me he had had a cablegram from his wife in America but she had not stated the name of the boat she was coming by, so he did not know whether he should have to go to Liverpool or stay in London.'

'It is just like a woman,' Murray, that genial man of the world, had said.

Murray said that all his references were in America and it would take a fortnight to three weeks to get them, but references were waived on immediate payment of the month's rent in advance. Murray just put his hand in his pocket and pulled out a handful of gold and notes and asked: 'Which will you have?' Ward implied that he had found the gesture somewhat ostentatious. But perhaps there was method in Murray's manner of payment. He always appears to have paid in cash. Even Florence never saw a chequebook. Presumably he had only one account and presumably it was not in the name of Mackie.

Wherever Murray obtained his funds, he must have had a fairly large sum when he came to Eastbourne. The rent of the house in Enys Road, the cost of living and a servant's wages must have been at least £6 a week, at today's values nearly £400.

During the next four weeks Murray spent much of his time in Eastbourne. He was for the most part with Edith at Enys Road, for he slept with Florence at Anniston Road only once and never at Whitley Road. But what is remarkable is that these three houses were all within a short walking distance of each other. The sisters might have run into each other. As it was summer, was it not likely that they would both wish to take their children to the beach? Was Murray not concerned about this? What if they met? Surely the game – if game it was – would be up. Did he enjoy some kind of balancing act? Was he a reckless risk-taker? What was the purpose of running such risks, especially as he seems to have genuinely loved his three children and both of the sisters?

Mrs Hutchins was engaged at Enys Road on 29 July to do the cooking and assist with the housework. She commented on how happy her new employers seemed. Mr Mackie, she said, was always playing with the baby girl and she never saw him in a temper. They always seemed to have plenty of money. Edith had told Mrs Hutchins that they had just come from America and, possibly explaining why they had no visitors, said that most of their friends lived in Scotland. Now these were absolute untruths and there is no explanation for them. Why did Edith tell such blatant lies to Mrs Hutchins? Just like her sister, she went along with Murray's constant false names and there arise inevitable questions. Why did both sisters accept the falsehoods? Why did they promote them? Is there more to this tale than we can ever divine? In Mrs Hutchins's opinion, Edith was of a very nervous temperament: she told Mrs Hutchins herself that everything got on her nerves. Was there some even deeper underlying tension in her relationship with Murray that has never emerged?

On Friday 16 August Murray told Mrs Hutchins her services would not be required after the next day. She understood they were going away for a time but that he was awaiting a confirmatory telegram. He said they intended to leave Eastbourne by the 9.30 a.m. train on the Saturday but there was a delay as no telegram had arrived. The cook last saw Edith in the house at about two o'clock on the Saturday afternoon and understood that they were still awaiting the telegram. They had not received it up to the time she left.

Some time after Mrs Hutchins left, Edith Murray and her child, the one-year-old Josephine, met their deaths at the hands of Robert Hicks Murray, who placed their bodies in the small front bedroom. It became obvious to the police that Murray did not kill his four victims and wound Florence all at the same time. They were convinced that he killed Edith and her child on the Saturday afternoon or evening. What remained of her clothing indicated that she was in outdoor dress when she was killed. The killing had taken place in the bloodstained bedroom. She had then been carried, fully dressed, along with her child, into the room later destroyed by fire. There was to be some speculation that the Saturday afternoon victims might have died from knife wounds as no gunshots were heard before the Monday morning and a small bloodstained knife was discovered, but this was never resolved.

After the Saturday murders Murray had called on Florence and told her that he was unable to take her to London that night. Was he clearing up, cleaning up the house? He said that he would call for her the next day. But when he did collect her at Whitley Road it was not to take her to London. Instead they were to spend the night in the house which she described as 'so old, so dark, so big and so lonely'.

And we know what happened there.

At about one o'clock, when Florence was in bed with the children, Murray came in without his jacket. His shirt sleeve was heavily bloodstained. He said that he had cut his finger cutting bread. Tired and unwell with a sore throat, Florence fell asleep, cuddling her children, but she was aware throughout the night that Murray was restless, walking about the house, coming into the bedroom from time to time.

Shortly after five o'clock Florence asked him, as he was up and about, to get her a cup of tea. He went downstairs and she dozed off again. Suddenly she was aware of him in the room, aware of him leaning over the bed, aware of him speaking to her, saying something like 'Come here'. And then there was a loud report. He had shot her in the neck.

Florence recounts what happened: 'I jumped out of bed screaming. My baby boy suddenly awakened and said, "Oh Mammy." I rushed out of the room and he fired at me again, the bullet hitting me again in the neck. I locked myself in a cupboard in the third bedroom. From there I heard more shots and groans and the moving about of things. "He's murdering my children," I cried and ran screaming to the front door. But no one came. Again I thought of my children and rushed upstairs. The sight was too hideous. I cannot talk of it. There were my poor darlings in the fire. I saw them.'

The flames were all around the babies, too fierce for her to attempt to save them.

Florence knew that her two children had been murdered. What she did not know when she had arrived at the house the previous night was that her own sister and the one-year-old niece she had never seen were already dead, their bodies in the locked bedroom which was now blazing.

Then the police came and the firemen and all those others who had been alerted by the shots and the screams and the smoke.

And after this the bodies of Murray, Edith and her daughter were identified.

So really, what about this man Murray who called himself Mackie or Morris or Stirling? What about this man who really did not own any of those names? What about the man who was known to his wives and many others as Murray but who in reality was differently named? Within days after the appalling events at Enys Road, a letter and photograph from Scotland Yard to Eastbourne police confirmed his true identity. The man's name was Robert Henry Money. It is by this name that he will be referred to from now on.

Robert Henry Money was never in the army. His father was not a barrister from Watford. Nor was his brother. Nor was his sister married to a Captain Hunter. Nor was he a Scotsman, despite allegedly having a Scottish accent. He was born in Farnborough in 1879, his father a carpenter, and he had lived in Watford as a child.

At the resumed inquest on 18 September, Mrs Charlotte Frith, Money's sister, gave evidence. Mrs Frith had maintained constant contact with her brother and had seen him as recently as 10 August, when he had visited her. He had collected a letter. In 1907, still in his twenties, he had gone to live with Mrs Frith and after he had left, he had continued to have letters sent to her house, all in his rightful name. There were never any letters in any other name. On this last occasion he had given Mrs Frith a cheque for £40 for her to send on to his mother. It was in settlement of some money he owed her. Was this a man clearing up his last debts?

Mrs Frith told the court that she had no idea that her brother had used a variety of names. She had not known that he was married, had never heard the name Paler and had never met either of the Paler sisters. Her brother, she said, had formerly lived at Kingston, where he and her eldest brother, Alfred, were in partnership in a dairy business. Robert Money had sold his share about six years earlier. She was not sure if he had worked since, although he had implied that he was in some kind of business but she was not sure what kind of business it was.

Mrs Frith said that her brother had a little private money, and also some rents from houses in Kingston. She thought that he might have sold some of these recently but could not be absolutely certain. Money played his cards close to his chest in all of his activities.

Mrs Frith did not know where her brother lived or stayed when he was calling on her. He gave no reason for not giving his address and she never pursued the matter. 'He was a man and I could not question him on the point,' she told the Coroner, evincing a certain Victorian attitude to the relationship between men and women. She did, however, describe her brother as being always straightforward, honest, sober and good-tempered.

What Mrs Frith's testimony showed was Money's capacity to retain intact whatever persona he was pretending to. Even accepting that many men at the time had the edge on their women, it is nevertheless remarkable that he was able to conceal great swathes of his personal life from people very close to him.

But the major witness was Florence, who appeared in court on the same day as Mrs Frith. In the past month she had been shot in the throat by a man whom she imagined loved her, by a man whose real name she had never known.

And here was a key question and answer in the proceedings.

'Had he ever spoken as though he might take his own life?' the Coroner asked her, suggesting that serious financial problems might have led to the tragedy.

'He said he would never see us starve,' Florence answered.

Did she think this was seriously meant?

'I used to take it as a joke,' she said.

'He implied that he would kill you rather than let you starve?' came the question. 'Yes.'

But then Florence, and presumably Edith, had never suspected there would be any financial problems, for they always had enough cash.

The case of Robert Henry Money remains an enthralling mystery. Perhaps he could no longer afford his bizarre lifestyle. Perhaps at last his funds had run out. But this whole, tangled charade was all the more curious as he made no profit from the two women in his life. Neither of them had any cash. He was not raiding their assets. And there is no evidence to support suggestions that he was defrauding anyone else. It's a considerable problem trying to divine Money's intentions. And it is equally puzzling to work out why he chose to play his game with sisters, which was always likely to end in some kind of disaster. The most charitable motive for the murders that can be attributed to him is that he wished to save them all from desperate poverty. But surely matters were not as serious as that. And another query relates to the two women themselves, both of whom participated in his other game of using false names. How did they explain to themselves why they were engaging in these charades? Apparently all of his victims loved him and trusted him. Was he so plausible? Or so menacing? Was it love or was it fear?

And there is one final mystery attaching to Robert Henry Money. On the evening of Sunday 24 September 1905, seven years before the Enys Road tragedy, a girl was

The News of the World *continued to report the case, with illustrations. Sophia Money is seen top left, Florence, the survivor, next to her and Money himself (with two versions of his signature) on the right. Merstham Tunnel is pictured below.*

thrown out of a Brighton-bound train in Merstham tunnel. Her body was horribly mangled. Investigators found a gag in her mouth. The girl was 21-year-old Sophia Money and her murderer was never found. Her brother Robert, a dairyman at Kingston, went down to Merstham to identify the remains. Afterwards, some said that they noticed a strangeness in his manner and it was said that he complained that the police suspected him. But if they did, he was never asked about his movements on the Sunday night. Chief Inspector Fox at Scotland Yard said that he regarded Money's attitude to be satisfactory and that he did all that a brother might be expected to do in the circumstances, no more and no less.

Then came a life change. Shortly after Sophia's death, Robert Money sold his share in the family dairy. Six months later, Fox met Money again and was struck by the sudden change in both his manner and appearance since their previous meeting. Still jocular and well spoken, Money now looked less like a dairyman and more like a man about town.

By 1906 Money had used the capital to build six houses in Norbiton. He rented these out and thereafter seemed to have 'abundant money'. In the months before the

Enys Road murders, as Mrs Frith suggested he had done, Money sold all of the houses. Was there now, by 1912, a growing financial problem?

Inevitably, in 1912 the police had to reconsider Money's 1905 alibi but were unable to shake it. Ignoring the fact that there had been a gag in her mouth, they continued to assert that Sophia had committed suicide by jumping from the train.

Nothing of course indicates that Robert Money had anything to do with his sister's death. There certainly was no apparent motive. But the terrible mystery of Sophia Money has never been resolved. All sorts of possibilities come to mind. It would perhaps have been helpful to know precisely where he was on that Sunday night. Because Robert Money, fantasist and seeming all-round decent chap, was a multiple murderer, one who in the end did not mind who was sacrificed: bone of his bone, flesh of his flesh, his legal wife, his little children. All of them consigned to a pauper's grave at Langney.

Robert Henry Money, riddler.

9

WHEN TWO STRANGERS MET

Portslade, 1933

In the first week of November 1933 Albert Probert from Hove and Fred Parker, a Dover man, both in their twenties, met each other for the first time. What they had in common was that neither of them was in employment. Who knows, but if Probert had found work as a fitter and the sickly Parker had picked up some labouring, things might have turned out differently. It might be that they had scoured the 'sits vac.' pages, that they had knocked on factory doors, had called at Employment Exchanges. But it is likely that regular work did not attract them. And they ended up in Portslade.

On 7 November they took digs with Mrs Payne in St Andrew's Road. They admitted that they were rather short of cash but assured her they would soon be able to settle up with her. Mrs Payne, who had asked for fifteen shillings a week rent, presumably thought that they looked honest enough. Or it may be that she was so desperate for cash herself that she thought it worth taking the risk. Alas, when they left on 13 November they had paid off only seven shillings and sixpence of their bill.

On 11 November they were touting sweepstake-draw tickets round the shops in Portslade. A shopkeeper in Church Road bought a ticket and some time later the men returned to her shop and tried to borrow money from her, offering to leave an overcoat as security. Somewhere they had come across a vacuum cleaner and they had that item on offer, too.

Two days later, on 13 November, they were still trying to sell the overcoat at Mr Smith's shop in North Street, but he was not interested. Why not try Mr Bedford's shop? he asked them. He sold all sorts of things. He might be interested in an overcoat.

Quite late on that same evening, Probert and Parker arrived in Worthing, booking into lodgings in the High Street and giving the names of Franklin and Minor. They paid four shillings in cash for their room. The next morning they went to a gents' outfitters on Brighton Road and each bought a new suit priced at thirty-eight shillings. Probert's overcoat had a button missing and the tailor sewed on a new one for him. Then off they went, the two of them, resplendent in their new outfits, their old clothes parcelled up under their arms.

Probert and Parker spent one night at 9 York Road before their arrest. (Courtesy of John and Sarah Green. Photo: The author)

In the late afternoon they took new lodgings, this time at 9 York Road. They were certainly flash by now, though what their future plans were is unclear. As it turned out, they had little time to develop any plans.

On 15 November, Police Constable Lovell saw a man standing outside a photographer's shop in the High Street, just opposite Worthing police station. A second man came and joined the first. PC Lovell thought they looked suspicious. In what way? They were dressed smartly enough in their new suits. Even so, PC Lovell was instinctively uneasy about what he saw. It might have been the suits, their very newness, which alerted him. It might be that in those straitened times, men in brand-new suits stood out. If Probert and Parker had continued to wear the shabby suits they had worn when they arrived in Worthing only thirty-six hours earlier perhaps PC Lovell would never have noticed them. But now they did not blend in with the background.

The constable approached the men. What were their names, he asked.

Frederick Smith and Jack Williamson, they told him. They had just arrived in Worthing. They had just come down from Croydon on a lorry, they said. They were looking for work.

But PC Lovell was not convinced. Come for work? Back of a lorry? In those suits? He took them into custody and handed them over to Inspector Lewis. The men were searched and the Inspector found twenty-seven farthings in Parker's possession. The farthing was in use at the time but it was the coin of smallest value and rarely carried in large quantities. Odd to find so many in Parker's possession. Inspector Lewis, still under the impression that he was speaking to men called Williamson and Smith, questioned Parker about what he and Probert were doing in the town and he was told they were looking for work. But Parker was not especially forthcoming, remaining silent for up to ten minutes at a time. As Lewis pressed him for answers, Parker asked, 'Why don't you go and ask my mate? I don't see why I should give someone else away.'

Perhaps under pressure, Parker broke. His stubborn shell cracked. 'I don't see why I should not tell you,' he told Inspector Lewis at last. Admitting their real names, he continued, 'We knocked an old man out in a shop at Portslade on Monday night. It was a shop where they sold bankrupt stock and we took the money from the till.' Lewis now anticipated finding out about other robberies but he asked Parker, 'Do you realise the seriousness of this statement you have just made to me?'

Parker replied that he did. 'Yes. I want to get it off my mind. We decided to hold up a chap in a shop at Portslade. It was an old dirty shop of bankrupt stock. We both looked in the shop window to see that all was clear. After investigating we walked into the shop and spoke to the old shopkeeper. I then turned and locked the door. No one was passing at the time and I brought my revolver into play. The gun was not loaded but I had no other choice of making the old shopkeeper put up his hands. I held him up and the other chap with me – I don't want to mention his name – went around the counter and just knocked him out. I went to the boxes and we both took money out and put it in our pockets. The farthings you found on me are some I took from the till. It was somewhere about £6 that we both got from the till. We have both since bought new clothing at Worthing.'

Later that night, Inspector Lewis again spoke to Parker who told him, 'I wish it had been a bigger job. It was not worth doing for £6. He was an old miser. I thought we should have found buckets of money. We found money in the boxes but there was a padlock and I had to wrench it off. It was only by luck I found it.'

It was a simple admission from the frail, rather delicate-looking young man. He knew that it was only a matter of time before the police learnt of their breaking into the shop and stealing cash worth, at today's value, £260. He did not want to be blamed for knocking the old man down. And he did not know what Probert might be saying in his cell. He might be telling them an entirely different story. All right for Probert sounding tough on the outside, but what was he like when the police started asking questions? When Inspector Lewis told Probert that Parker had mentioned the robbery, he refused to say anything.

But unknown to Worthing police, for the past twenty-four hours police in Portslade had been busy. While suits were being bought and lodgings changed and while arrests were being made in Worthing, the police in Portslade were investigating a murder. On the night of 13 November, an eighty-year-old bachelor, Joseph Bedford, had been found seriously injured in his shop, just about the time that

Probert and Parker were moving into their lodgings in Worthing. The next morning the old man had died in Hove Hospital.

Bedford's shop stood on a corner site, its windows looking out to both Clarence Street and North Street. There was a sign on a slate reading 'Bankrupt stock – special' in one of the windows. The shop was jam-packed with all manner of articles – ironmongery, earthenware, tools, buckets, brushes, mats, china, pictures, books, keys, boxes. There was a glass case in which were two boxes, and in one of these the owner kept silver and copper and in the other, farthings.

When Police Constable Peters on his evening rounds noticed goods still stacked outside Bedford's shop, he was surprised. The old man usually took everything in about eight o'clock. The shop was in darkness and the constable called out, but there was no response. Then he heard a noise inside. Again he called out. The old man was deaf: perhaps he had not heard him. PC Peters flashed his torch through the glass panel of the door. The light lit up the old man standing by the counter.

'The light fell full across the face of Mr Bedford and I could see that it was covered with blood,' the constable said later. 'The next moment I saw him stagger backwards. He fell against gardening shovels resting against a showcase. I then forced the door and found Mr Bedford lying in a heap on the floor.' Bedford's face was battered beyond recognition.

The following morning, after Bedford died in Hove Hospital, Detective Chief Inspector Askew arrived from Scotland Yard to assist the local police. At the crime scene there were copper coins scattered over the floor and a bloodstained copy of the previous evening's newspaper. In the passageway leading to the kitchen there was a tooth, a pair of shattered spectacles, a tie and a detachable shirt front. There was also a bowler hat, its crown dented. Behind the shop counter, Askew found an overcoat button.

The police found a number of witnesses anxious to help. Bedford had been a kindly, well-liked man and they were horrified at what had happened to him. Alice Sandells, who at 5.15 p.m. had taken Bedford his evening meal as she had done for the past fifteen years, had called again at the shop at about 8.40 p.m. to post the evening newspaper through the letterbox. Another neighbour, Kathleen Russell, had been in the shop talking to Bedford at eight o'clock and had noticed two men outside whom she had not recognised. But Joseph Smith had recognised them as the two men who earlier in the day had tried to sell him an overcoat.

And now there came a phone call to Portslade police from the police at Worthing. They had a couple of men in custody. One of them had admitted to robbing a shopkeeper in Portslade a few nights earlier. They had apparently knocked the old man about. Did they want to interview the men? Yes, the Portslade people replied. The old man had died.

When police searched the room in which the men had been lodging in York Road, they found a revolver, more cash, including farthings, and Probert's heavily bloodstained blue suit. Later scientific tests would show the blood to be of the same group as Bedford's.

On 17 November Chief Inspector Askew went into Parker's cell and told him he was enquiring about Bedford's murder. Parker was agitated, anxious, wondering what to say, how to say it, how to get himself off the hook. 'You don't mean to say the old chap is dead?' Askew warned him that whatever he said would be used in court. 'Then I will tell you what happened,' he said at last. 'I didn't want the old chap hurt. I will take my part now but now that I know he is dead I will tell you who the other man is that I spoke about in my statement to Inspector Lewis. The next statement was made before I was enlightened upon the true facts. The man I spoke about is the man who is charged with me. I met him in the Church Army hostel at Brighton by accident. He told me that he had a job worth doing and when he put the question to me would I go with him, I said "No, it is not worth it." The job was on Cromwell Road and on the way we had a lift by a man named Hall. This man, Hall, handed Probert a revolver or gun. He also handed me a tyre lever. Probert said to me "Now we can get some easy money."'

Parker had already admitted in his statement to Inspector Lewis that he had been carrying a gun during the robbery. He now had to make sure that Askew did not think that he was inclined to use it. The statement continued, 'I said to him [Probert], "You don't know what you are saying." He said, "I don't care a hang." When he handed me the revolver I asked for the magazine to be taken out. Probert got mad and asked me why did I want the magazine taken out. Then I said, "Thank God it's empty."'

Throughout Parker's statement Probert was identified as the leader, the man with the suggestions, the more forceful personality. Parker was making it clear who should bear the responsibility. And of course, the 26-year-old Probert was Parker's senior by five years.

Now armed, they discussed another job. 'Probert asked if I would "do" a jewellers. I said that the shop was bound to have alarms all over but Probert said he was desperate. I tried to get him to talk sense. We walked round Portslade and we came to the shop [Bedford's]. I explained to Probert that it was a big risk and I would not take any part except holding the gun. Probert said that was all right.'

When they went into the shop it is probable that Probert began by offering the overcoat to Bedford.

'While Probert was talking to the old man I turned the key, already in the door, and coming back I told Probert that the old man was deaf and could not hear what we were saying, but if he did hear to hit him gently. I took the revolver from my pocket and asked the old man to put up his hands. He resisted at first and Probert struck him. Probert was leading him backwards and, as he struck, the old chap went down. Probert did not take any notice of what I said and kept on asking if I had got the money. I told him to put a scarf under the old man's head. He was knocking his head on the floor and I could hear that distinctly. I told Probert, "I have found the money" and he left the old chap and we left the shop together.'

As for the tyre lever, Parker said that Probert had gone to Albion Villas in Hove and had 'planted' it. And, he said, Probert had told him he had lost a coat button.

Parker's statement took two hours to complete. Lewis then took it to Probert's cell. Albert Probert, though undeniably nervous, was made of sterner stuff than Parker. When Lewis read it to him, Probert resolutely denied any involvement in the affair. Where news of the old man's death had thrown Parker off balance, Probert held out for an hour, saying only, 'The statement made by Parker in which he refers to me being with him at the shop of Mr Bedford is absolutely untrue. I have been asked to say where I was on Monday evening, November 13, and I have nothing to say.'

If on 17 November Probert stoutly denied being with Parker at the shop, after a night's sleep and time for reflection he changed his mind. According to Inspector Lewis, he called him to his cell to ask him a favour. 'I want you to go to get that tyre lever which Parker said we did the job with. I can prove it was not done with that. I was going to use it but we did not after all. We did it with that gun. I can prove that I was there. It is all lies about the tyre lever. You will find it in the garden at Albion Villas, near the railing. Put your hand through. I think it is near a tree. I want you to get hold of that lever and then you will see that it is all lies what Parker said how we did it.'

This, the policeman said, was an admission that Probert was present when the old man was killed. Later it would be withdrawn. The tyre lever was recovered from 16 Albion Villas in Hove.

Sir Bernard Spilsbury, Home Office Pathologist, sketched by George Belcher for Punch.

Probert and Parker were then taken to Portslade and charged with murder. Within the hour they appeared before Hove magistrates and were remanded. In December and January they appeared several times before being committed for trial. At these hearings Parker collapsed in the dock on eight occasions. Once he fell back into the arms of a policeman and another time, just as he was describing the multiple head and facial injuries which had led to Bedford's death, Sir Bernard Spilsbury ran from the witness box to assist Parker. At the Lewes Assizes, facing the murder charge, he collapsed again.

The courtroom at Lewes is small, compact and wood-panelled, but it is a theatre and you are as close to the actors as you could ever wish to be. There have been great dramas enacted here, fewer comedies and only the occasional farce. The giants of their profession have all appeared here: Marshall Hall, Norman Birkett, Sir Travers Humphreys and many others have topped the bill at Lewes. This place has seen the worst of villains. Sidney Fox who murdered his mother; John George Haigh, the acid bath murderer, who claimed to have drunk his victims' blood; the rather handsome Patrick Mahon and, rather less dandified than these, Norman Thorne who buried his former girl-friend in the chicken run; Field and Gray in their cheap suits, the pair who did away with seventeen-year-old Irene Munro on the Crumbles at Eastbourne. But there have been scores of others, the wicked, the infamous, the depraved and the downright vicious. At this session of the Assizes, though the law will be its customary dapper self – some of the greatest legal luminaries will appear – the two in the dock will be at the lower end of the market. Who would have thought that they were strangers to each other at the beginning of November of the previous year and that within a fortnight of their meeting they would find themselves facing a capital charge?

The Law Courts at Lewes, 2005. (Andy Gammon)

The four-day trial of Probert and Parker was opened on 13 March 1934 before Mr Justice Roche. Sir Henry Curtis Bennett KC and Mr Maxwell Turner appeared for the prosecution. Mr John Flowers KC with Mr Thomas Gates appeared for Probert and Mr J.D. Cassels KC with Mr Alban Gordon for Parker.

Sir Henry Curtis Bennett opened by saying that Parker had admitted to being in the shop when Bedford was so badly beaten. He said that if two persons went out for the purpose of committing a robbery, knowing that violence was likely, and if one of those persons used violence and the other simply stood by as Parker said he had done, then that person was just as guilty of murder as the person striking the blows. From the outset, the Crown was making no concessions to Parker.

J.D. Cassels KC.

The *Brighton & Hove Herald* commented that 'there was a stir in court when Sir Bernard Spilsbury, the famous pathologist, was called', and later there was a shudder when the great man produced a human skull to illustrate Bedford's injuries. Spilsbury attributed his death to shock, the result of multiple injuries to the face and head. He suggested that a heavy instrument had been used. If, as seemed to have been the case, the old man had worn the bowler hat when he was attacked, then the blow must have been delivered with considerable force. The fractures to the nose, cheeks and upper jaw were caused by a number of separate blows. Bedford had suffered neck injuries, too, from a hand round his throat.

The statements of Parker and Probert, which had not been heard in the magistrates court, were now produced for the first time.

When Parker took the stand he was asked about his claim that Charles Hall had given Probert the gun and the tyre lever. Hall of Hartington Road, Brighton, said that he had known Probert for some time. He denied giving either man a revolver or a tyre lever.

Parker was asked in detail by his counsel, Mr J.D. Cassels, about the robbery. He claimed that Hall had suggested robbing Bedford's shop though there was evidence that the shop had been quite innocently pointed out to them by another shopkeeper. The gun was empty, Parker said.

'I held the old man up with a gun and told him that we had come for money,' Parker said in reply to Mr Cassels. 'He put up his hands eventually and I stepped back for Probert to tie him up. We had tied my scarf and Probert's together for that purpose. I thought that we were going to carry out the whole thing by merely tying him up.' But then Bedford had resisted.

'Before the old man put his hands up Probert let out a terrific right which landed near his ear. I could not get near them. The old man went down and there was a kind of struggle.'

Probert was banging Bedford's head on the edge of the desk and Parker told him to stop. Bedford got up and Probert caught him by his shirt and pushed him along the shop, hitting him. Finally, Parker tried to stop the violence. Parker said, 'I told Probert that the old man had had enough and to give it up. He told me to keep my mouth closed and said that if I did not he would do the same to me as he had done to Mr Bedford.'

Q: Had there been at any time any arrangement which you had made that the old man should be treated violently?
A: No.
Q: Had you known that there was to be a violent assault upon Mr Bedford in any way would you have joined in this adventure?
A: Certainly not.

When Parker was cross-examined by Sir Henry Curtis Bennett, he admitted that on the day before the robbery, Probert had said that it might be necessary to use violence.

Q: So you knew the day before that the man you went to rob the shop with was a very violent man?
A: In a way, but I never thought he would carry out what he said he would do.

This concluded Parker's evidence and, supported by two policemen, he returned to the dock.

When it came to Probert's turn in the witness box, police crowded round him, fearing that he might attack his co-defendant.

Sir Henry Curtis Bennett KC.

Probert now challenged the statement attributed to him and went back to his original denial of ever being in the shop, and for the first time he produced an alibi. He and Parker, he said, had left each other at eleven o'clock that morning and did not meet again till nine o'clock that evening. Examined by Mr Flowers, he said that the night before the murder they had exchanged clothes. Parker put on Probert's blue suit and overcoat and he wore Parker's brown jacket, flannel trousers and brown overcoat. When in the evening they met at Portslade station as they had arranged to do, Parker was excited, wanting to get out of the town. It was a wet evening and Probert, already soaked, borrowed Parker's overcoat. When he put it on, he said, he noticed that there was a missing button. As for the blue suit with blood on it, he admitted it belonged to him but said that Parker had borrowed it on the morning of the murder because he was meeting someone from London who might give him some money and wanted to look his best.

Cross-examined by Curtis Bennett, Probert said Parker's story was totally false. There had been no discussion between him, Hall and Parker about breaking into a shop. He said that Parker did not speak to him at any time about an attack on Mr Bedford and that he had not suspected anything wrong.

Probert said he was in Brighton all day on 13 November. He had sold Parker's brown overcoat to a man in a snooker hall. He had had lunch, had visited the Palace Pier, had gone to the library. At about six o'clock he had passed the Jubilee Clock Tower. He had walked slowly towards Hove, sheltering once or twice because of the heavy rain, and arrived at Hove Town Hall at about ten minutes before eight o'clock. He had caught a bus to Portslade station and met Parker who told him he had managed to get £3 10s, which they shared. According to Probert, he was not in Bedford's shop but his clothes were. But this account of Probert's had never been introduced at the magistrates hearings. It was all new.

In his closing speech, Sir Henry Curtis Bennett described it as a remarkable case. Out of the mouths of the accused, he said, came their admissions of guilt. 'You have had here, the picture of one man accused of murder going into the witness box and telling a story and inculpating his fellow prisoner. I am going to submit that when Parker was in the box he gave evidence on his own behalf which was a confession that he had committed murder. You have also had the picture of the other accused person going into the witness box and denying that he had anything whatever to do with the crime – denying that he was wearing the clothes he was said to be wearing, denying that he had benefited from robbery.'

'If that story of Probert's is true,' he asked the jury, 'do you think it is possible he would never have mentioned it to a soul, outside possibly his solicitor there, until he went into the witness box yesterday? That is a story which you cannot believe.'

Mr Cassels, defending Parker, said he proposed to put forward the possibility of a verdict of manslaughter in certain circumstances. He said if a person indulged in excessive violence which could not have been anticipated by his companion and which he himself had never anticipated – and the victim died – so far as the passive man was concerned it might reasonably be called manslaughter.

'I am afraid', Mr Justice Roche told him, 'I shall have to tell the jury that the proposition is not correct in law.'

Well then, said Cassels, was it not more reasonable to come to the conclusion that Bedford's fall backwards at the time when PC Peters shone his torch into the shop might have played a very important part in the death of the old man? 'But for that fall, might not Bedford have lived?' he asked.

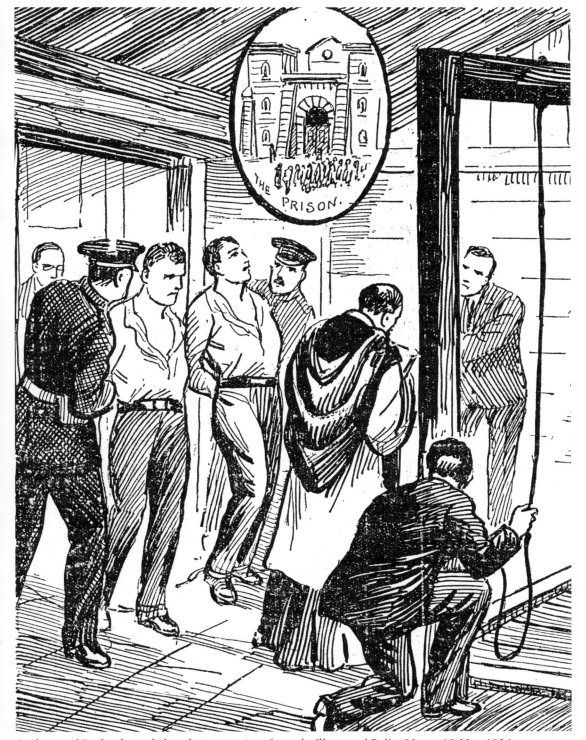

Probert and Parker being led to their execution, from the Illustrated Police News, *10 May 1934.*

Mr Cassels said it was not part of his duty to assist the prosecution to establish the guilt of Probert, but when Probert went into the witness box to suggest that Parker was telling untruths then it was his bounden duty to address himself to Probert's position in the case. The jury might well have to consider whether there was not a great deal in the failure of Probert to provide witnesses to his day out in Brighton.

Mr Flowers for Probert also suggested that Bedford might have been frightened by the sudden flashing of PC Peters's lamp through the glass door. Possibly the shock caused him to fall, fracturing his skull. He asked the jury to believe Probert when he said he was not there. But if they did come to the conclusion that he had taken part in the robbery, Mr Flowers submitted that it should be a verdict of manslaughter.

It was a desperate defence by both Cassels and Flowers. Both tried ingeniously to save their men. And failed. The jury took only thirty-nine minutes to return a guilty verdict. Asked if he had anything to say why judgment should not be pronounced against him, Probert declared his innocence. Parker seemed to be wishing to say something at the same time but before he was able to speak Mr Justice Roche, who had apparently not seen the movement of his lips, proceeded to pass sentence.

And up in the gallery, throughout the four-day ordeal, sat a forlorn young woman in a green dress. It was Probert's wife.

Both men appealed unsuccessfully. They hanged at Wandsworth on 4 May 1934, the first double execution there since Field and Grey.

10

THE DANCING WAITER

Brighton, 1934

Under the twinkling coloured lights and Chinese lanterns, the band plays 'I'm Confessin' that I Love You', and Toni, master of the slow foxtrot, breathes the words into her ear. Sherry's dance hall, with its hint of cheap perfume and sweat, is his world, where he can pick up girls, tell them how nice they look, because he is a gentleman. Perhaps he'll invite one of them round for a cup of tea maybe. It's only a small place, he'll say. But it's all right for the present. Some of the girls know him well enough because he's here many an afternoon and evening. And they like him with his rather coarse handsome looks, his brilliantined hair parted down the middle and his little pencil moustache (that is if he hasn't shaved it off again). And maybe it's the Italian in him that some of the girls like. Toni Mancini, it's sort of romantic, girls think, as he whisks them round the floor. Not that he is Italian. Nor for that matter is he Toni Mancini, but this is Brighton, that old nicotine-stained playground, that old gin-fumed palace, and you can be who you like here.

Sometimes these days they ask him about Violette, say they haven't seen her around recently. And he tells them she's gone off to France with another man, but at other times the story changes and she's gone to France on a two-year contract as a

Two 1934 advertisements for Sherry's.

dancer though some might think that at forty-two she's past that kind of entertaining. Anyway, he told Joyce Golding that he didn't want Violette back because she was always nagging. She'd rowed with him in public, right in front of all the customers at The Skylark, and he didn't want that again. She'd gone to Montmartre, he told Joyce.

Away from Sherry's, perhaps at the Regent where he tangoed away some of his days, other people asked Toni about Violette, where she'd got to. Down at Aladdin's Cave, the amusement arcade near the pier, he told one of the skittle-alley attendants

Violette Kaye. The press dubbed her 'the girl with the dancing legs'.

that he was glad she was gone. She was 'a fucking prostitute' and he'd kept her for three years, he said, and she'd just walked out on him. Not an entirely true account of their relationship. Violette, certainly a prostitute, had kept Toni so that he had time for the dance halls, the billiards saloons, the pubs and the cheap cafés in which he spent his days.

Another time in Aladdin's Cave, Toni told some of the fellers there that he had had trouble with his missus and had given her the biggest hiding she had ever had in her life. 'What's the good of knocking a woman about with your fists? You only hurt yourself. You should hit them with a hammer the same as I did and slosh her up.' 'Hit them with a hammer' – what a thing to say!

Anyway, Violette had gone but that didn't interrupt the dancing and all the other pleasurable little activities that made up his life. Everything went on as usual, him out in his highly polished dancing shoes and keeping smart because if you have Toni's tastes you have to look right. You're dancing to 'Body and Soul' or 'Little White Lies' and you're so close to the girls you can't afford to not to look your best. One thing, though, he decided to change his digs in Park Crescent where he and Violette had recently lived.

The move to 52 Kemp Street, in a shabby little thoroughfare near the railway station, was done very cheaply on 14 May. No removals van was needed because there wasn't really very much to move. All he had to do was enlist the help of a couple of friends, Johnny Beaumont, the blind piano-accordionist, and Tom Capelin, washer-up at the cheap and cheerful seafront Skylark Café ('Well worth trying – our 1/- dinners – children 6d') where recently and quite against the trend Toni had taken up employment as a waiter, outside tout and if-need-be bouncer.

Nevertheless, though most of his possessions packed easily into cardboard boxes, there was an extremely heavy trunk to move. 'What you got in here, then? A body?' Capelin asked him. 'Well, it's all the crockery and silver,' Toni had answered. 'It's heavy stuff.' So they had to find a handcart to take the load.

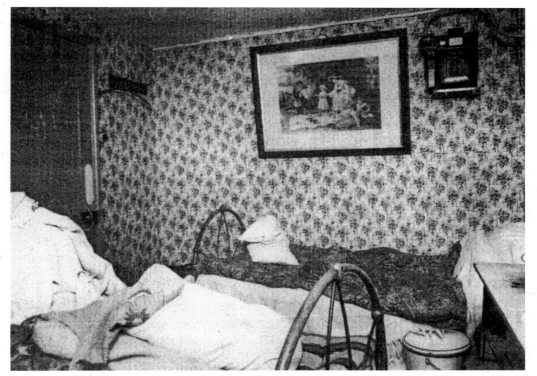

The basement room at 52 Kemp Street. (Reproduced with the permission of the Chief Constable of Sussex, copyright reserved. ESRO ref: SPA 11/3/4)

The new basement flat was tiny and the trunk, covered with a pretty patterned cloth, had to do service as a chair, which visitors must have found uncomfortable. And there was such a funny smell about the place. Toni told some of his visitors that Mrs Barnard, the landlady, did not open the window during the day though they might have wondered why Toni did not do that himself. He told one enquirer that somebody had died in the room and that it had been disinfected but because of the hot weather the smell would not go out. Another time, and these enquiries seem to have been regular, Toni claimed that his sweaty football boots were responsible. Incidentally, Queens Park Rangers had been keen to sign him on. Or so he said, never being quite able to resist a spot of embroidery.

Neither the landlady nor her husband had any sense of smell and so they did not share the visitors' queasiness. Nevertheless, when she went into the room one day, Mrs Barnard noticed brown fluid seeping from the trunk. Deeply perturbed, she asked Toni about it but he was able to allay her fears. It was, he told her, a unique blend of French polishes which would enhance the floorboards rather than disfigure them. Delighted, she asked him for a quote: how much would it cost to do the whole floor? When she had gone Toni considerately dried the floor and placed a sack under the trunk.

Of course, it must be obvious that Toni has an unusual problem. Let's not discuss how it was that Violette Kaye died because there are versions of that, but what is not in any doubt is that on the night of Thursday 10 May 1934, Violette died in the flat in 44 Park Crescent. She had suffered a violent blow to the head. Let's not at present try to work out exactly what happened. Just let us find her on the floor and let us imagine that Toni does not know what to do, for he is a man with some form. He is afraid, he will later say, to send for the police.

But he seems to do nothing immediately. He sits for hours, pondering. Rigor mortis has almost set in when he decides to make some attempt to conceal the body. But with the limbs stiffening it is no easy task fitting Violette into the wardrobe. Then, over the hours, while he lies in bed, the body in the wardrobe, as it relaxes, squeaks and groans. And in the night he recalls that Violette's sister, Olive, is coming down to Brighton, coming to stay with them, in the next day or so.

Early the next morning Toni sends a telegram. 'Going abroad. Good job. Sail Sunday. Will write. Vi.' But the telegram misspells Olive's address – 'Plantatinate' instead of 'Palatinate Terrace.' Olive will later wonder about that. Such a funny mistake for her sister to make.

Later that day he was dancing with Lizzie Atterill, a waitress at the The Skylark. In fact he took her back to Park Crescent where he introduced her to Mr Barnard, the landlord, as his sister. He gave her a green dress and a fawn hat, both of which had been Violette's. She hadn't had enough case-room for them, he said. Days later, treating her to cod and chips at the Aqua Café near the Palace Pier, he complimented Lizzie on her appearance in her new dress. Toni always knew how to compliment the ladies.

There was other urgent business for Toni in those days so shortly after Violette's death. After all, he had lost his principal source of income and something had to be

Toni Mancini at ease on Brighton seafront.

done. He tried to encourage one or two of the girls he knew to work for him. He'd look after them, he told them. Joyce Golding was one of those he invited round to the flat but she understood what he was after. 'He invited me for the simple reason that he knew what I was,' she said. She was having none of it.

For the move to Kemp Street on 14 May, Violette had been transferred to the black trunk which Toni had bought for ten shillings. And then it was back to normal, back to The Skylark and best of all to Sherry's, to the Regent, to the girls.

The weeks pass by. Toni dances, Violette moulders in Kemp Street, and Brighton is preoccupied with another body, this one also in a trunk but found on 17 June, a very warm Sunday, at Brighton railway station. The room attendants have been aware for a day or two of a smell coming from a trunk and on this day, with the heat overpowering, they decide to do something about it. There is at one point the half-jokey suggestion that a forgotten joint of meat has been left. But they call the police and it falls to Edward Taylor, a Brighton detective constable, to open the trunk. The stench is overpowering, coming from a brown paper parcel tied with sash cord. When the layers of paper are pulled away there are a woman's remains, a torso, a head, limbs. She was pregnant and in her early twenties.

A massive and thorough police investigation followed. Chief Inspector Robert Donaldson of Scotland Yard and Detective Inspector Pelling of Brighton headed the investigation but they could never find out who had deposited the trunk. Despite innumerable telephone calls and more than 12,000 letters and the pointing of fingers at scores of suspects, despite scrutiny of missing persons registers and searches of left-luggage offices throughout the country, despite interview after interview, and even despite, Brighton being Brighton, the offerings of clairvoyants, numerologists, seers and water diviners, the police never satisfactorily solved the case, though some have suggested that a well-connected Hove doctor had botched an abortion. The victim was never identified, although the press, with their unfailing originality and sensitivity, were to describe her as 'the girl with pretty feet'.

Toni Mancini, 'the dancing waiter'.

But Toni Mancini's heart missed a beat on the Monday afternoon when he heard the newspaper sellers shouting out that a corpse had been found in a trunk. He was relieved no doubt when he returned to Kemp Street to find that the trunk was still there, its pretty patterned cloth undisturbed. Nevertheless, the sudden activity over the unidentified woman led the police to Toni Mancini. One of Violette's regulars had called at Park Crescent and had been told that Toni and she had left. In the circumstances he was suspicious and went to the police. On Saturday 14 July Toni was interviewed by Chief Inspector Donaldson, giving his real name, Cecil Lois England. He was able to satisfy the detective that he had nothing to do with the body at Brighton station. And anyway, he told Donaldson, Violette had gone abroad. Perhaps Donaldson required little persuasion. 'The girl with pretty feet' was only in her twenties whereas Violette Kaye was forty-two. Toni was released. But it is likely that even now police spent some time delving into the sleazy background of Violette and Toni.

And so should we, for Violette was not just a body in a black leather trunk. She had had what might be described as an interesting life. Since her teens she had appeared in a variety of chorus lines including 'Miss Watkins' Rosebuds' and 'Parisian Pinkies', performing in a variety of tacky music halls and adopting as her stage-name Kaye rather than using her real name, Saunders. Later she had been part of a dance duo, 'K & K', which had some success, but their cabaret and theatre career trailed to an end. Perhaps it was drugs, perhaps it was drink, certainly towards the end of her life Violette was heavily into both. Now she was a faded, worn, little peroxide blonde, no longer able to persuade theatrical agents of her worth. When she met Toni Mancini in London in 1933 she was a convicted prostitute. He told her that he had no work and she agreed to be the breadwinner.

In September 1933 Violette and Toni, her pimp, moved to Brighton, he only twenty-six, her junior by sixteen years. While she pounded her beat on the seafront, he danced. When she brought clients home or when regulars like Charlie Moores or the one they called 'Hoppy', the one with with the limp, or 'Darkie' came round, he made himself scarce. For the next six months, there was a constant moving from one set of dingy rooms to another until, finally, they ended up at the basement flat in Park Crescent calling themselves Mr and Mrs Watson. At the beginning of May, Charlie Moores, the most generous of Violette's regulars, a man she referred to as 'Uncle', was taken away to a mental home and in the same week, for the first time since they had met, Toni found work at The Skylark. Perhaps this was an indicator that Violette's pulling power as a prostitute was also fading.

And as for her dance-hall Lothario, he was perhaps less of the hard man he claimed to be than a self-deluding waster. The name he was born with in Deptford – Cecil Lois England – did not have enough about it to impress. So he transformed himself, depending upon the circumstances and situation, into Toni Mancini or Luigi Pirelli or Anthony Luigi or Jack Notyre. According to the criminologist Jonathan Goodman these aliases were not intended to help him avoid the police and were no more than symptoms of the Valentinoesque dream-world he lived in. Toni had served in the RAF for two years and later had worked as a waiter in Leicester Square, but there had been no sign of any sustained attempt to work in the past three or four years. He dropped hints that he had been involved in protection rackets with the Sabini gang in London, claims that he had moved to Brighton when he became a marked man. But the records show convictions for stealing silver and clothing in London and for loitering with intent to commit a felony in Birmingham. Not really a hard man's sheet.

And not an intelligent man's record either. How long did Toni originally intend to leave the body in the trunk? Did he ever have any plans to rid himself of it? Or did he just intend to dance the days away, hoping that all would work out in the end?

The interview with Donaldson on Saturday 14 July seems to have made up his mind. He needed to get away, to lose himself in London. And perhaps he was stampeded into going off when he learnt that painters were to begin work in the flat on the Monday, but the planning was random, feckless and irrational. What occurred in the next few hours indicates much about this hopeless character. That evening, Saturday, he went to Sherry's where he talked to Joan Tinn, one of the dancing instructresses. He told her that he was leaving Brighton and going back to London but Kemp Street, he told her, was going to be famous. We can imagine the knowing wink, the smirk. He was going to be famous, too, although he did not say that to Joan.

After this he met two friends, spending the rest of the Saturday night with them. He told them that he was going to London to see 'some of the boys' and his father. They all three went to Kemp Street to help with his last-minute packing and one of them commented on the smell in the room. Was he keeping rabbits? No, Toni told him. It was 'them upstairs'.

After that they went to an all-night café and then to Preston Park station where he caught the train. There'd be quite a lot said about Kemp Street in the newspapers before long, Toni told them. He'd have his photograph in all the papers. Just wait and see.

The following day, Sunday, Toni was in London, evidently short of cash as he was obliged to pledge a pair of trousers and two shirts. But Toni cannot help being Toni. He meets a girl, seventeen-year-old Doris Saville. They go to Lee Green, she listening and giggling, he smiling and spreading the charm. And then, after some hours, on the way back he asks her if she can keep a secret. 'It is about a murder. If I happen to be caught you ought to dictate this story to the police.' He wanted her to say that they had met on Brighton seafront, that they had gone to tea with a woman at Park Crescent who had told them she was expecting three men to come and see her. They had left the woman and when they had returned to the house they found that she was dead. Doris was later to explain that Toni wanted her to provide him with an alibi. This tale was later to come up in court and it is of little importance save to point up the feckless manner in which Toni Mancini conducted his affairs. As if a seventeen-year-old girl, a virtual stranger, was likely to shield him successfully in a court case.

But by the Monday the police were seeking him. The painters, working on the outside of the flat in the absence of the owners, were quite overcome by the smell. It was so overpowering that they reported it to the police, who broke in. And it was Detective Constable Edward Taylor, he who had opened up the trunk at Brighton railway station only weeks earlier, who had the ill fortune to be called to this house, to perform the same task. In a corner of the room, near the fireplace, was a large black trunk, bound with thick cord. DC Taylor probably expected to find Miss Pretty Feet's missing parts inside. But no. Here, along with some clothing, including a mouldy and bloodstained overcoat, was a whole body, doubled up, and now infested with inch-long maggots. The mothballs which had been placed in the trunk had in no way softened the raw stink that rose from the trunk.

Unlucky police. They now had two unrelated trunk murders on their hands. But lucky in the sense that they had a suspect for what became known as 'the Second Brighton Trunk Murder'. Police were told to keep a look-out for Toni Mancini.

In the early hours of Tuesday, policemen in a patrol car at Lewisham recognised the man wanted for questioning in connection with the trunk murder at Brighton. They stopped the car and approached him.

'Excuse me, sir,' one of the officers asked him, 'do you happen to be Mr Marconi?'

'Mancini,' he says, knowing there is no way out for him.

Later, under questioning, he agreed that he was the man they were seeking but he swore that he had not murdered her.

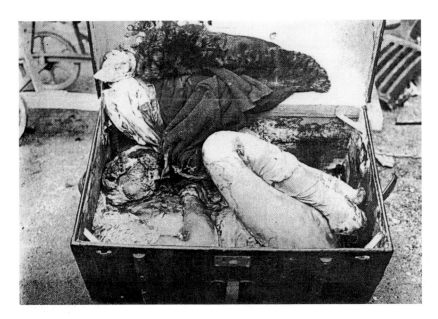

Violette Kaye's body in the trunk. (Reproduced with the permission of the Chief Constable of Sussex, copyright reserved. ESRO ref: SPA 11/3/4)

'I wouldn't cut her hand,' he said. After all, why should he? As he said, 'She has been keeping me for months.'

Toni Mancini's arrest was on all the front pages, so that when he arrived at Brighton police station on the Wednesday morning there was a crowd waiting for him. There were mounted police in Market Street ensuring that matters did not get out of hand. He was now a real celebrity, a monster, greeted by locals and holiday-makers, ferociously baying for his blood. He was the trunk murderer, they had no doubt. Yet there were those who just knew him to be innocent, many of them young women who boasted that they had danced with him and some who claimed an even more intimate knowledge of the arrested man. 'Hello, Toni, keep your pecker up,' they called out, and 'Don't worry, Toni, all will be well' and other optimistic comments.

Later in the morning he appeared before Brighton magistrates, charged oddly enough under one of his improbable aliases, Jack Notyre. He was charged as follows: that he 'feloniously, wilfully, and with malice aforethought did kill and murder one Violette Saunders between the 7th and 15th May, 1934'.

On 10 December, after a series of hearings at the magistrates court, Toni Mancini – the name which for convenience we shall stay with – appeared at the Sussex Assizes at Lewes before Mr Justice Branson. The case was identified by the police as 'Brighton trunk crime number 2' to distinguish it from the unsolved case of the woman whose dismembered body had been left in Brighton station in June. The popular press referred to the principals as 'the dancing waiter' and 'the girl with the dancing legs'. Let it not be thought that pepping up a story is a post-war invention.

Inevitably there was enormous interest in the case and applications from the public for admission tickets far exceeded the court's capacity of 100 seats. And when Toni arrived at the court he was greeted by a huge and generally hostile crowd.

Mr J.D. Cassels, KC, assisted by Quintin Hogg, KC, appeared for the Crown and the formidable Norman Birkett KC for the defence.

The prosecution case was that Violette had died from 'shock – depressed fracture of the skull'. This was the finding of Sir Bernard Spilsbury, the enormously influential pathologist whose opinion had led to the conviction of many murderers. Violette's head he had found much bruised. She had been killed, Spilsbury said, 'by a violent blow or blows with a blunt object, eg a hammer, causing a depressed fracture extending down to the base, with a short fissured fracture extending up from its upper edge'. Two small bruises on the left side of the skull indicated that Violette was lying upon a hard surface at the time when the blow was struck.

Sir Bernard Spilsbury, Home Office Pathologist.

A hammer? The Crown now produced a hammer-head found among the rubbish in the cellar at 44 Park Crescent. It had been examined by Dr Roche Lynch, the Home Office analyst, who was of the view that it had been passed through fire, presumably to rid it of blood.

The basement room of 44 Park Crescent. Violette Kaye's body was hidden in the cupboard. (Reproduced with the permission of the Chief Constable of Sussex, copyright reserved. ESRO ref: SPA 11/3/4)

On the afternoon of 10 May, the day on which it was suggested that she died, Violette had turned up at The Skylark Café and had started a blazing row with Toni in front of customers. He had tried to quieten her down as she accused him of over-familiarity with Lizzie Atterill, who was present. Eventually he either persuaded or forced her to leave the premises. He told Lizzie to take no notice. Violette, he said, was jealous. And she had never been seen after that day.

The prosecution pointed out that Toni had been at great pains to explain Violette's disappearance but that he had never been absolutely consistent in the reasons he gave. She had left him; he had thrown her out; she had gone off with another man. As for the misspelt telegram sent to Olive Watts, Violette's sister, just a day or two before she was due to arrive in Park Crescent on holiday, this was clearly written by Toni. A graphologist concluded that the telegram was written by the same hand that wrote out the menu cards for The Skylark. And what about his introducing Lizzie Atterill as his sister to his landlord, only a day or so after Violette's death?

Did not all Toni Mancini's conversations and his actions from 10 May until his arrest point irresistibly to the conclusion that he had murdered her? In the prosecution's view there was no necessity to prove or establish a motive. The outstanding feature of the case was concealment of the body from 10 May. Was it not contrary to human instincts and human nature? Did this not indicate the man's guilt? Toni Mancini had said he was reluctant to go to the police but he had found a body and had called in no help. Nor did he send for a doctor. Instead he had spent the night removing all traces of blood and then hiding the body in the cupboard. And next morning he was alert enough to take the precaution of stopping Violette's sister from coming to the flat, after which he had bought the trunk and moved house.

Norman Birkett opened the defence with a protest about the 'wickedly false stories' circulating about the case and about his client. But he made no attempt to disguise the fact that the trial would introduce to the jury and the public 'a class of men and women belonging to an underworld that makes the mind reel'. No good covering up the truth, he seemed to be saying. We will give you raw, unpalatable facts. And Toni Mancini, he is telling his audience, is a man of that class and his story is essentially one which has often been told before and disbelieved.

Spilsbury's evidence had to be dealt with. It was Spilsbury, that prosecution darling, who swayed juries. Toni Mancini's acquittal would depend on demolishing the pathologist's certainties.

The hammer, for instance. Under cross-examination by Birkett, Spilsbury was asked, 'Which end of the hammer do you say the accused used?'

Spilsbury did not hesitate. 'It might have been both ends but more probably the smaller end,' he said.

But did this not contradict the evidence Spilsbury had given before the magistrates? There he had said that the fractures in the skull had been caused by something like the bigger end of a hammer. If the pathologist's evidence could not be trusted, well . . .

Norman Birkett (wearing spectacles) and his colleagues at Lewes Assizes during the trial.

And the fracture, what about that? Was it not the case that a fracture from a fall was often indistinguishable from that caused by a blow? Was it not at least possible that Violette had fallen down the steps of the basement? Might she not have hit her head on the projecting stone or window ledge? After all, 44 Park Crescent was approached by a flight of steep and badly worn steps. At the head of the steps, which had an iron railing, was a stone brace and at the foot a projecting stone window-ledge. He thought she might have tripped over the brace. But no, Spilsbury insisted, her injuries came from a hammer.

'Are you really telling members of the jury that if someone fell down that flight and came upon the stone ledge he would not get a depressed fracture?' Birkett asked, nagging away at this point.

'He would not get this fracture,' the pathologist replied just as doggedly.

Here Mr Cassels intervened. 'If there had been a fall such as has been suggested in this case, would you expect to find injuries only to the head and no injuries to other parts of the body?'

'No, I should certainly expect to find bruises on other projecting parts.'

'In your view,' the judge interposed, 'is it possible for this woman, having received the injury which you saw, and having gone through a period of unconsciousness, to recover sufficiently to walk to the bed or undress herself or do things of that sort?'

Spilsbury would have none of it.

'It is possible to have happened after a depressed fracture, but in this case it is quite clear it had not happened.'

But why not? It was a crucial matter in the trial. Birkett had edged some doubt into the minds of the jury members. Had Violette, having taken drugs, tripped down the outside steps and fallen down, hitting her head? And had she then staggered to her feet and found her way inside? After all, Dr Roche Lynch, the Home office analyst, was of the opinion that before her death Violette had taken a quantity of either opium or morphine considerably in excess of an ordinary medicinal dose. Did not Thomas Kerslake, a witness who spoke to her outside the house at four o'clock in the afternoon on the day of her death, think she had been taking drugs? She was twitching convulsively and in a highly nervous state.

And then supposing it was true that she had been struck a blow which had killed her. Why should it necessarily be Toni Mancini who was guilty? Kerslake thought he heard voices inside the flat that afternoon. Who might that have been? Was that her murderer?

At no point in the trial did Birkett dispute the fact of the concealment of the body. That was not an issue as far as the defence was concerned. The man in the dock had most certainly hidden away the body. But he was frightened. A man with a criminal background might be more readily suspected than one who had never been in trouble with the law.

In the witness box Toni, at times overwrought, gave an account of what had happened on the night when he returned home from work at half-past seven. The front gate was open, he said, but the front door was locked and he had no reply when he rang the doorbell, and he had been forced to climb in through a window. Violette's coat lay on the floor of the bedroom. She was lying on the bed, clutching the sheets with one hand. There was blood on the pillow and also spots of blood between the door and the head of the bed. His solution was to hide the body in the wardrobe. He spent the night in the armchair and no, he assured the court, he had never seen a hammer.

As for the telegram he had sent to her sister, what else could he do? What for that matter could he have said to all those people who had asked him where she was?

In a simple and telling series of questions from Birkett, Toni, clearly distressed, reveals himself as a man who loves his woman despite her faults and who suddenly finds himself in a most awful predicament.

'Did you live with Violette Kaye at Brighton?'

'I did, sir.'

'Where did she get money?'

'She was a loose woman and I knew it.'

'Did she appear to be in fear?'

'Yes. That's why we were always on the move.'

'Was she often intoxicated?'

'Often.'

'How did you get on together?'

'Strange as it is, I used to love her.'

'Had you any quarrels?'

'None.'

'Does that cover the whole time you were together?'

'Every second she was alive.'

'How did she behave when she came to The Skylark Café on Thursday, 10 May?'

'She was staggering a little. She wasn't herself. She was affected by something. All week she had been rather strange.'

'What time did you get home that night?'

'About half-past seven.'

'What did you do when you saw her lying on the bed?'

'At first glance I thought she was asleep. I caught hold of her shoulder and I said, "Wake up." Then I saw blood on the pillow and on the floor.'

'When you found she was dead why didn't you fetch the police?'

'I? I fetch the police? Where the police are concerned, a man who's got convictions never gets a square deal.'

Birkett took him through the whole strange story. The buying of the trunk, the move to Kemp Street, the escape of some of the liquid which had stained not only Mrs Barnard's floor but his own clothing too. As for her being in constant fear, which led to their frequent moves, Toni recalled a time when they had been attacked. When they had first arrived in Brighton two men had called on them, presumably asking for protection money. Toni had refused, had sent them off. Then he told how one evening he and Violette had been walking along the seafront. 'A young man came across and slashed my face with the razor blade and tried to slash her. Of course, I knocked him down. He got up and ran.' He said he went to the police about this and asked for protection; he said they were being blackmailed by local gangsters. But he let the matter drop because police said he could not prove they were being blackmailed.

And no, it was not true that he had said that Violette nagged him. Nor had he ever beaten her and it was untrue that he had ever said in Aladdin's Cave that he had bashed her. And there were other falsehoods. He had never asked Miss Golding to come to live with him. He thought that she and another Brighton prostitute, Miss Gordon, had been asked to make damaging statements about him. And he hadn't said anything about Kemp Street becoming famous.

But it was in his closing speech that Norman Birkett was at his most impressive. 'There is a feature of this case that has never been in dispute – the concealment of the body and the lies told to explain it,' he told the jury. 'But concealment and lies, remember, are not murder. Consider the position in which this man found himself.

When he went home from work that night and found the woman dead, his immediate reaction was one of sheer terror. "I shall be blamed," he thought, "and I cannot prove my innocence." So he went out; he walked about; he turned over this dreadful situation in his mind; and when he returned he put the body in the cupboard and nailed the door upon its hideous secret. Members of the jury, once that is done, all the rest follows. Once you have started on the road of lies, you're compelled to keep on telling lies. There is no going back.'

The jury must not forget the possibility that she had fallen down the steps leading to the basement flat, but supposing they concluded that it was murder? Well, he went on, 'Violette Kaye was a prostitute. That man [pointing to Mancini] lived on her earnings and I have no word to say in extenuation, none. But you must consider the world in which such people live and the dangers to which they are exposed. Isn't it reasonably probable that in this woman's life – an unhappy, a dreadful, an unspeakable life – blackmail may have played a considerable part? Somewhere in this world are the people whom Kerslake heard speaking in the flat when he went there on 10 May. The finding of the body was proclaimed from the housetops. Those who were in the flat that day – they had a tale to tell. But not a word, never a word.'

The case was 'riddled with doubt', Birkett told the jury. There was no motive as the couple were generally on good terms. The prosecution had neglected to pursue the possibility of a morphine dose. And why, if Toni had killed Violette with a hammer, had he not got rid of it? Why leave it lying around for two months for the police to pick up? And what of the possibility of enemies in Brighton? Might they not have come to murder her?

Birkett concluded, 'I ask you for, I appeal to you for, and I claim from you, a verdict of not guilty.' At this point he paused and then looking at the jury again he added, 'Stand firm!'

And they did. They did stand firm. For five days they had listened to the sordid tale of a petty crook and a prostitute. All the evidence pointed to Toni Mancini's guilt. But the jury returned a not-guilty verdict.

'Not guilty, Mr Birkett? Not guilty?' the bemused client asked, for he had been rescued from what had seemed a sure-fire guilty verdict. Not that everyone agreed with the jury's findings. Toni Mancini was smuggled out of the court by a back door to avoid a crowd ready to lynch him. Whatever the jury had said, there were thousands who had no time for Toni Mancini. And Norman Birkett, whose *tour de force* had saved him, referred privately to his client as 'a despicable and worthless creature'. The case was one of the greatest of his career but it had 'given me very little pleasure'.

In the following summer Toni toured fairgrounds in a sideshow act, sawing a lady in half. A variation in his act was that instead of putting the lady in the customary wooden box, a long, black trunk was used. In this case the lady in the trunk was his new wife.

In September 1935 Toni Mancini was sentenced to three months' imprisonment with hard labour on a charge of theft in Trowbridge. A 22-year-old woman charged with him was bound over. They had gone into a jeweller's shop and had looked at

Mancini's acquittal, as published in the Illustrated Police News.

some watches, and when they had left a gold watch was missing. The defence was that the girl picked up the watch in the street.

Not until 1976 did Toni Mancini resurface into public view. He contacted Alan Hart of the *News of the World*. After forty-two years, he said, he wanted to put the record straight. He told how at the trial the idea had been conveyed that he was only a petty criminal with no history of violence. But now he wanted to admit that he had been a ruthless thug, working in clubs for London gangs. There is no reason to believe that he was doing other than fantasise.

But another part of his story does seem true. He admitted to the murder of Violette. On the day on which she had made a scene at The Skylark he had taken her home. She was drunk and heavily drugged. In the house they had had a row. He had thrown a coal hammer at her which had hit her on the head and killed her. He had not intended to kill her.

But how had the jury ever believed him? The case against him had seemed so watertight. 'I rehearsed my lines like an actor,' he told Hart. 'I practised where to place my hands and when I should let the tears run down my cheeks. It might have been cold and calculating but remember my life was at stake.'

And it worked. But was this the true story? You never knew with Toni.

Some years later he gave an amended version of what occurred. As he had earlier said, he and Violette had argued after they returned from The Skylark but now it was she who had picked up the hammer and he, struggling with her, hit her head repeatedly on the fender.

In 1986 Toni Mancini, now living under another name, and apparently happily married and well respected locally, made another admission. He had not killed Violette. He had been totally innocent all those years.

The choice is yours. You have three accounts to select from. Only one seems to be highly unlikely, but you never know with Toni.

11

THE ARUNDEL PARK CASE

Arundel Park, 1948

Let's just follow this young woman, this 27-year-old Joan Woodhouse, as she leaves the YWCA hostel in Blackheath at half-past eight on this lovely Saturday morning in 1948. She has just said goodbye to another resident, Nicole Ashby, who hopes that Joan will have a good week-end up in Barnsley, her home town. There does not seem to have been much of a rush this morning because Joan is an organised sort of person. She prepared everything last night, ironing her clothes and packing her case.

Joan is making for the Underground, which will take her to King's Cross station, where she will catch the 10.10 train to Doncaster. Then she will have to change for Barnsley. She was up in the north quite recently when she wasn't well, stayed nine weeks or so with her aunts at Bridlington, but when she felt better she came back to work. But now, as it is a Bank Holiday, she has Monday off and she won't be due back at work at the National Central Library in Malet Street, Bloomsbury, until Tuesday.

She is a small girl, only five feet tall, and not unattractive. Under her beige coat she is wearing a Paisley-patterned dress, a pearl necklace and blue sandals. In her blue-lace gloved hand, she is carrying a brown leather handbag and the small blue case she packed last night. Over her arm is her green, hooded macintosh because although the forecast is good you can never tell what the weather might be like in Barnsley. Somewhere along the way she buys a newspaper. Perhaps she reads it during the journey but at some point she folds it carefully and puts it in her handbag.

But hold on. This is odd. She does not go to King's Cross. We next pick her up in Victoria station. She buys a railway ticket, a single, to Worthing. What has happened to the visit north, where she was supposed to visit her father? It's inexplicable because she is such a good daughter and he is such a good father, and it seems that they were anxious to see each other again. He will obviously want to know if she has recovered fully since going back down to London. And so will her two aunts, who dote on her. And naturally they will be concerned if she doesn't turn up because they haven't forgotten the suicide attempt last Easter. Half-hearted it might have been, a few sleeping tablets, not enough to kill her, but it does indicate that at that time Joan was emotionally frail. And so there are going to be some very disappointed and mystified people up north when Joan does not arrive home.

At Worthing, Joan goes to the left-luggage office and deposits her suitcase. She puts the ticket in her handbag. So where now? Perhaps she goes into the town. It's impossible to say, but she next appears in Arundel and she probably travelled there by bus. The place is crowded and the little librarian is somehow and somewhere lost in the mass of sweating Bank Holiday visitors.

At about two o'clock on this sweltering hot day she calls in at a chemist's shop in the High Street and buys a bottle of Lembar. While the chemist will not remember her, he will recall selling a lemon barley water to somebody that afternoon. Sometime after this, a Miss Dibley, who is visiting friends in Arundel, notices a young woman in a blue-patterned dress walking by herself towards Arundel Park.

Joan Woodhouse with friends in London, c. 1948.

Joan knows this park, loves it. When her aunt, Ida Sheriff, lived in Worthing, she used to bring her here. And there is a place away from the crowds that she knows, a quiet spot, secluded. She leaves the path and climbs the hill on her right. It leads to Box Copse where the beech trees and the bushes will give her some shelter from the heat. And when she gets there she opens out her macintosh on the ground and rolls her beige coat into a pillow and as she removes her dress, perhaps she reflects on the people at home because she knows she will never be in Barnsley tonight. It is impossible.

Does she feel guilty, this hard-working, responsible, intelligent girl? People whom she loves are expecting her later in the day. But she cannot hope to get to Barnsley now. Think of the journey. Southern Electric from Arundel and stop off at Worthing to collect her case. Then take the next train to Brighton and change for Victoria. After that, cross London to King's Cross and take the train to Doncaster, which is what she told Nicole Ashby she intended to do earlier in the day. Or maybe she could go from St Pancras and catch a train to Sheffield and then take a local train to Barnsley. But neither option, especially considering the railways in this immediate post-war period, will permit her to reach home this night. And she knows this surely. Yet she has made no arrangements for accommodation for this evening. Not at Worthing where she left her case, and neither at Arundel nor at Littlehampton. Nowhere has she reserved a room. What are her plans?

Here is this well-brought-up, sensible woman, an organised woman, meticulous in her habits – why, even the clothes she has taken off are neatly folded – who sits in the dappled sunlight, miles from Barnsley, miles from the YWCA, seemingly having made no preparations. It is on the face of it extremely out of character.

And finally she fades from our view . . .

On Tuesday 3 August, when Joan was due to return to work, there was no sign of her at Malet Street. What did her colleagues think? That there had been some problem with travel? That she was ill again and might be away for several more weeks? Nothing was done about her absence until the following day, when she was again away from work and the head librarian called the hostel to find out if she was ill. But there was no word of her. Nobody knew anything. She still had not returned from her stay in the north. On the Thursday, Joan's father confirmed that Joan had not come home for the holiday. She was officially recorded as a missing person on that day. But no one could have imagined that she had gone to the south coast and on to Worthing. It was mystifying. Had she fallen out of a train? Had she stopped off at one of the stations between Kings Cross and Doncaster?

In the late afternoon of 10 August a local man reported to the Arundel police station. He had found a woman's body in Box Copse. He had seen a handbag first, then a pile of clothing. And then he had seen the body.

The missing woman's body lay on a wooded slope in Box Copse, a favourite spot for courting couples in Arundel Park. After ten days in the open, the face was unrecognisable and there was some decomposition of the head, although the rest of body was very well preserved.

Police reconstruction showing clothes worn by Joan Woodhouse on the day of her murder.

She had lain there in the seclusion of the dense copse, only partially clothed, wearing pink camiknickers, a brassiere, an elastic suspender belt, stockings and sandals. Round her neck was a string of pearls and on the third finger of her right hand she wore a ring.

Higher up the slope, twelve yards or so from the body, the raincoat was spread out and a beige overcoat at one end had been folded up to serve as a pillow. Nearby her dress was neatly folded. In a brown leather handbag were a powder compact, a green and gold lipstick case, a left-luggage ticket from Worthing station, a pair of white-framed sunglasses and an envelope containing a single Luminol sleeping tablet. At her side was an empty bottle of lemon barley water.

When Dr Keith Simpson, the Home Office pathologist, arrived on 11 August he was unable to give a precise date for the death. The recent ravages of weather, a mixture of torrrential rains and intermittent hot sunshine, had accelerated decomposition. Simpson's best estimate was that she had died between eight and ten days previously. A newspaper in her handbag, dated 31 July 1948, strongly inclined all investigating the case to favour ten days.

Simpson concluded that she had been strangled. He noted fingertip-type bruises on the muscles on both sides of the neck and the right horn of hyoid bone. There was also some minor bruising on the scalp and over the spine and hip. On the thighs and round the entrance to the vagina there was further bruising, hinting at a violent penetration. There was a ball of pubic hair at the top of the vagina which could have been carried there only by the insertion of a finger or penis. There was also pubic hair on the brassiere. The body was infested with maggots which had removed all signs of semen.

Keith Simpson viewed this as a sex murder and this was the conclusion of Detective Chief Inspector Fred Narborough, the Scotland Yard officer called in to assist the West Sussex CID. Any theory that it might have been a robbery was soon dismissed. The pearls were intact, the handbag containing pound notes untouched. From the beginning the police wondered if she had been accompanied by a man friend. Had there been some preliminary sexual activity which unexpectedly turned sour? Or had she simply lain down to sunbathe and been chanced upon by a total stranger? There were some small indications that despite her frail build she had put up a brief struggle, that she had managed to escape just a few yards down a little pathway, tearing her stockings and scratching her legs as she ran. Or was she strangled on the macintosh and then carried to a less conspicuous place? And there was nothing in the way of fingerprints on the bottle. They had been washed away in the previous week's downpours.

But there was a diary and this gave impetus to the most extensive manhunt on the south coast in post-war years. The diary contained the names of about 150 people, most of them men whom she had met in the last six months, although there were no diary entries of any kind in the fortnight before her death. What sort of girl kept lists of men's names like this? Was there some secret history? Had the unassuming librarian some other hidden life? Narborough and his team set out to interview all of her friends and acquaintances and to seek out every stranger who might have seen her during the holiday week-end. Narborough had an idea that somewhere in the background was a unknown lover, that Joan had a secret assignation with him, that she had met him in Worthing or Arundel and that they had gone together to Box Copse.

A team of 100 detectives checked every name in the diary. Narborough was convinced that her murderer was among them and as a result of one of these leads he spent three days talking to a man in the Birmingham area, but this was a dead end. At least two men, one of them in Rhodesia, confessed to the murder and wasted police time. And there were so many other dead ends. It turned out that in the main the men named in the diary were librarians, from all parts of Britain, all members of a professional association of which Joan was honorary secretary. Others were friends and relatives.

But what about sightings? Had anyone seen Joan Woodhouse in the company of a man? There were hundreds of responses to the police appeal. Yes, some had seen her with a man. But equally there were those who swore that they had seen her alone.

And what about the party she had attended in north London on 13 July? Who was the 'exceptionally nice man' Joan met, the man she had mentioned to friends? He was just another red herring. As were the claims of some Worthing hoteliers who thought that she and a man friend had stayed at their hotels over the Bank Holiday week-end.

The landlord of The George and Dragon at Burpham, three miles from Arundel, claimed that a girl answering Joan's description called in for a drink at about 12.20 p.m. on the Saturday. There was a man with her, a thirty-year-old, of medium height and build. Even allowing for some inaccuracy in the time, it was obvious that this was not Joan because at about that time she was leaving her case at Worthing station.

The manhunt extended to hotels and boarding houses, to reception staff, waiters, cleaners and still-room maids; to every British Railways employee at Victoria,

Worthing and Arundel; to taxi drivers, van drivers, bus drivers and conductors; servicemen and secretaries in the neighbouring towns and villages. The aim was to interview every male over the age of fifteen in Worthing and Arundel, though whether this was achieved is debatable. This was a massive operation searching for an unknown killer who had been in the area between ten and eight days before the body was found.

By the middle of September, however, the investigation had achieved nothing to help find Joan's murderer. But it did reveal something of her character and background. And it showed very firmly that some press commentary had been grossly unfair in leaping to conclusions about her, a semi-naked woman with a list of names in her diary. For she was very proper young woman, a former Sunday School teacher and a deeply devout worshipper.

Only months earlier she and her boyfriend had talked about marriage, but there were irreconcilable religious differences and Joan could not commit herself to a man whose beliefs were not as deeply held as hers. The rupture in their relationship had pained her, which was why she had suffered a breakdown, why she had made a futile attempt at suicide.

An inquest held on 13 August, only three days after the finding of the body, was adjourned in order to give the police time to find the murderer. But after six weeks of fruitless search, Narborough began to think that he was on the wrong track. Perhaps it was some stray remark, but at some time during the manhunt period one of Joan's aunts mentioned how much she loved to sunbathe. It would not have been surprising, she said, for Joan to find some out-of-the-way spot to enjoy the sun. This set Narborough's thoughts in a new direction. What if she had gone to Box Copse on her own? What if she had felt herself to be away from the world, safe from interruption and had stripped off? And then someone had found her? This was how, after what he called the 'six wasted weeks', Fred Narborough began to think. Had some local man followed her? Or had he, a total stranger to Joan, just happened by? Had he raped her and then strangled her?

By the time the inquest was resumed on 22 November it was clear that Narborough had a suspect but insufficient evidence to charge him. This was 24-year-old Alan Wade, who lived at Offham near Arundel. He lived with his parents in a grace and favour house on the Duke of Norfolk's estate and worked for a local builder as a house painter. He had given evidence of finding the body at the adjourned inquest on 13 August. Wade had also explained that he had been walking in the park on the day he had found the body. He had been off work that day with a poisoned hand but in the afternoon he had left home at about two o'clock. He had gone to his allotment over at Burpham and had put some time in there and then had walked home, taking a short cut through the park. It was then, passing through Box Copse, that he saw the body. He had run down to the lodge, borrowed a bicycle and had cycled to the police station to report what he found.

Now, at the renewed inquest, the real interest focused on Wade, who was informed by the Coroner that he was not bound to answer any question that might incriminate him. How odd such advice must have seemed. This was an inquest, its purpose simply to find out how Joan Woodhouse had died. Wade had not been charged and yet he was being informed of his legal rights. In fact he had turned up at court with his solicitor. 'The jury would like to know if it is normal that this witness should be legally represented if he is only giving evidence about finding the body,' the foreman of the jury stated, and was told by the Coroner that the jury must use its own judgement on that matter. It was as good as acknowledging that Wade had a case to answer.

Wade was asked by Mr C.V. Porter, for the police, 'Did you tell the police you were in the park on 31 July?'

'Under pressure, yes,' he replied, 'but I am not sure of the day.'

But had he not told the police that he was in the park on 31 July? Had he not made a statement to that effect?

'I said I must have been, owing to the fact that they said I had been seen there.'

Mr Vincent Jackson, representing Wade, asked, 'When you found this woman did you as soon as possible go to the lodge, where you are very well known, obtain a bicycle from there, and immediately go to the police to give information as to what you had found, and did you subsequently give them every assistance in your power?'

'Yes.'

The real problem was, as Chief Inspector Narborough admitted, that the police had been able to trace only two persons who thought they had seen Joan on the afternoon she met her death. At present, they were unable to produce enough evidence to justify the institution of criminal proceedings against anyone. Inevitably, the jury returned a verdict that Joan Woodhouse had been murdered by some person or persons unknown.

Narborough's frustration at the result was evident in a report which he wrote after the hearing. It concludes, 'In my opinion the murderer is Alan Wade. He is fully aware that there is insufficient evidence to put him in the dock, and acting on the advice of his solicitor, he will not admit to any further questioning by the police except in his presence.' He was sure now that Wade would never confess to the murder and held out little hope of a future conviction unless further concrete evidence were found.

Joan's family was devastated by the result of the inquest. They had spoken to Narborough, who had informed them of his suspicions that Alan Wade was responsible for the murder. The aunts, Mrs Sheriff and Mrs Blades, were determined to bring the matter to a conclusion, to have the guilty man in court, to have Wade in the dock. If Detective Chief Inspector Narborough could find insufficient evidence, if he was from now on unable to devote time or detectives to the case, then they would seek help elsewhere. First of all, they offered £500 for information. But there were no results from this. Then in August 1949, fourteen months after the murder, they recruited a retired CID sergeant from Bridlington. Tom Jacks's experience of murder cases was limited. This was only the second murder he had dealt with; his private detective agency was principally engaged in divorce work. But the aunts had faith in him and Jacks certainly worked hard. For the next fourteen months he devoted himself to the task. And at two guineas a day, the equivalent of £50 today, the aunts spent most of their savings. In the course of his investigation, 55 days of which he spent in Arundel, he interviewed 200 people. Jacks's tireless activity whipped up the interest of the press in the case. An article by Wade in the *Sunday Mirror*, complaining that local people were treating him as if he were guilty of the murder, saying that his life and that of his fiancée were being ruined, only served to keep the case in the public eye. While Tom Jacks did not produce strong evidence, because the case was cold by the time he got to it, his energetic enquiry and the report he sent to Scotland Yard ensured that positive action followed.

Chief Inspector Fred Narborough.

In February 1950, Fred Narborough having retired, still unwaveringly convinced like Jacks that Wade was the murderer, the Yard now assigned another senior detective from the Murder Squad, Detective Superintendent Reginald Spooner, to reopen the case.

Spooner had before him the reports from Chief Inspector Narborough and Keith Simpson, the pathologist, as well as the one that Jacks had sent to Scotland Yard. He gave immediate consideration to the three statements Wade had made to Narborough. They contained important inconsistencies. Spooner called Wade for interview with a view to clarifying them.

In his first statement Wade had told Narborough that on the day he found the body he had been to the doctor's with his poisoned hand. On the way home, he said, he had taken a short cut through the copse. But that was patently untrue. No short cut from the surgery to his home would have taken Wade through Box Copse.

The second statement had corrected this. This time he said that he had gone into the copse because he was poaching rabbits. He had not admitted this before because it might have come to the ears of the head keeper and there might be trouble. It might even end up with his parents being thrown out of their grace and favour cottage.

And in a third statement Wade admitted that the reason he had gone to the copse was to indecently expose himself to two small girls. Wade already had a conviction for indecent exposure.

There were other features that Spooner addressed. Turning again to the first statement, he asked Wade why, when he had said that on 31 July he was painting at home in the morning and that in the afternoon he had gone to a shop in Arundel and later to see a film in Littlehampton, he had not mentioned being in the park that day. Wade had told Narborough that he was uncertain about the times and dates. He gave the same reason to Spooner.

But the second statement contains some telling information. 'I went to Swanbourne Lodge and spoke to the lodge keeper,' he told Narborough, 'and to the man who runs the boats on the lake. I went to the walnut tree and as I was walking along I saw a girl walking ahead of me. She was about 30 yards ahead of me. I hurried to see if I could catch her up but I did not catch her up. I spoke to some people I knew and then I noticed the girl had gone up the valley . . . I walked up the slope towards Box Copse in the direction the girl had taken. I saw she had turned round. I said, "Good morning, lovely day." I got no reply. She hurried away down the slope. I sat down, and later I walked down to see if I could see her, but she had passed out of sight. I never saw her again. I walked round the lake back to the lodge. She seemed to be very nervous. She seemed to look at me and hurry on. The facial resemblance and build of the girl I saw was similar to that of Joan Woodhouse . . . Although all the facts about this seem to point to me, I am innocent and know nothing whatever about the death of Miss Woodhouse.'

Narborough had shown Wade a picture of a group of girls. Was the girl he saw in the park on the photograph? Wade pointed to Joan Woodhouse and began to cry. 'If that was Joan Woodhouse I saw, then I must be to blame for what happened to her,' he said. It was a cryptic kind of remark and it was not at all clear what Wade intended by it. Narborough asked him to explain it.

'Well, it was me that frightened her and she ran into the copse where someone found her.'

Later Wade retracted his identification of Joan, saying that he did not think it was the girl he saw. It was someone similar in face and build.

Dubious stuff, certainly. But not enough to charge Wade with. Not even with Wade's admission that he was in Arundel Park on 31 July 1948, that he followed a girl who answered to Joan's description and that in the park, in a highly excited state, he masturbated.

Frequently it is the victims, their circumstances, their histories, which resolve puzzles of the kind now facing Spooner. The detective went back to study Joan through her diary and through discussions with her friends and relatives.

Spooner's enquiries revealed a shy and reserved woman with no sinister history, no dubious background secrets. She was extremely religious, a lay member of an Anglo-Catholic organisation, the Company of the Sacred Mission. Religion was not an adjunct to her life; it was central to it. Religion was the most important element of her being. Two years before her death she had written the code by which she tried to live. 'My Way of Life' outlined a regime of prayer, meditation, retreats and interior mortification. A fifth of her earnings she had decided to give as alms.

But what happens when belief falters, when doubt assails the believer and all those comforting certainties are no longer in place? There was some evidence that in recent weeks Joan had begun to lose her faith. For one so strongly committed to the religious life, it must have caused anxieties of the gravest kind; it must have seemed to her like a bereavement. Spooner was totally convinced that Joan had been utterly wretched in the last weeks of her life, so bereft that she could not come to record in her diary in the last fourteen days the devastation she was experiencing. Perhaps the ending of her relationship with her boyfriend, the result of their inability to reconcile their religious differences, had led to the loss of belief.

And so to depression and so, thought Spooner, to suicide. The single tablet of Luminol in her handbag, why just one tablet? Where were the rest? Had they been washed down with a draught of Lembar?

But what about the conclusions of the pathologist? Simpson was pre-eminent in his field, a man of considerable experience, highly respected. And now Spooner rejected Simpson's assertion that Joan had been raped. As far as Spooner was concerned, the body was too decomposed when it was examined for there to be any certainty that intercourse of any kind had taken place. And why had there been no bruises on her arms? Rape victims struggle and they are restrained by their attackers, who grip their arms and wrists. But there was no sign here of any violent struggle. And what about the button on her camiknickers? It was still fastened. Did that seem likely if she had been raped? Wasn't the button of the knickers likely to have been torn off?

Despite the glaring inconsistencies in Wade's statements, despite the fact that the circumstances pointed towards him, despite Narborough's and Simpson's reports, Spooner concluded that Joan Woodhouse had committed suicide. He believed that on her way to King's Cross on 31 July she had changed her mind. Perhaps she had been suddenly weighed down by some great sense of desolation, of being absolutely overwhelmed by what she perhaps recognised as a burden too heavy to bear. Was that the moment, somewhere on her way to the Underground, that she made her awful decision? She would go south, not north. And when she ended up in Victoria she had already made up her mind. She would end it all. She bought a one-way ticket. And at Worthing she realised that there was no point carrying her case. She would have no further need for it. And she would go to Arundel Park which she had loved to visit with her aunts when she was young. And as she walked into the copse, almost in a kind of trance, her legs were scratched and her stockings torn. What did any of it matter? And there it ended.

Broadly, that was Superintendent Spooner's thinking when after six weeks he handed his report to the Director of Public Prosecutions, who announced that nothing from this second investigation justified further action.

Unsurprisingly, Professor Simpson was displeased with the detective's conclusions, which disputed the post-mortem findings which he had presented at the Coroner's court. While he was unable to explain why it was that the necklace remained intact around her neck, he did answer the observation that Joan's arms were not bruised.

Simpson was of the view that the reason for this was that her arms had been entangled in her clothing as she struggled. This is not convincing simply because Joan was not wearing much clothing when she was found. And what assailant, after raping and strangling his victim, would put the disarranged clothing in a tidy pile before making his escape?

It seemed, now that the case was over, that unless something turned up, some new and striking piece of evidence, some confession from the murderer stricken with remorse, the files would be locked away for ever. But Joan's father had the same determination as her two aunts. He was unwilling to allow the matter to rest. In August he applied to the Arundel magistrates for a private warrant against Alan Wade. It was the first such application since 1865. It was granted and Wade was arrested and remanded in Brixton Gaol.

On 19 September 1950 Wade appeared before the magistrates. Mr J.S. Bass, representing the Director of Public Prosecutions, warned the court when opening the case for the prosecution that the evidence was wholly circumstantial. There was not a single piece of evidence that directly proved the case against Wade. Admittedly, the accused man had had the opportunity to commit the murder, but that in itself was insufficient to commit him to trial. The instinctive reluctance of the DPP to bring this case was very evident from the beginning.

Bass referred to Keith Simpson's report on how Joan had died and then moved on to speak of Wade's varying statements about his movements on the day Joan was last seen alive. He had at one point denied being in the park and on another occasion had admitted being there. And then, on 10 August, he had found the body, he said. There were witnesses who saw him go into the park at half-past four. Half an hour later he was seen walking away from the copse. Now, the copse was only fifteen minutes' walk from the gate he had come in by which suggested that he had walked straight to the body.

'It is a remarkable thing,' Bass said, 'if the finding of the body was by chance and you may wonder if it is a true statement. You may think this man killed this woman on 31 July and seeing nothing about it or the finding of the body, could not resist his curiosity any longer.'

And there are cases of murderers who return to the scene of their crime to look at their victims. In 1939, for example, Charlie Cowell returned on five consecutive days to check that Ann Cooke was still where he had left her in Pondtail Wood near Albourne. John Holloway and Ann Kennett, too, returned to Lovers' Walk on several occasions.

What was important to the prosecution case was any witness who had seen Wade and Joan Woodhouse together on 31 July. But the only witnesses who made the claim were totally unconvincing. Mrs Nellie Petley, who had contacted Jacks during his investigation, said that over the Bank Holiday week-end she, her children, and her daily help, Mrs Beatrice Bidwell, had picnicked several times in the park. On 31 July they had sat near the walnut tree at the end of Swanbourne Lake. Mrs Petley said that she saw Wade with a young woman. Though they were talking, it had not seemed a friendly conversation. In fact neither had seemed very happy. Mrs Petley had asked the man the time but he had no watch. After they passed by the couple sat on a slope about 200 yards away and then they had got up and left, though she could not say where. Then they disappeared.

Vincent Jackson, representing Wade, asked Mrs Petley about a letter she wrote to Tom Jacks during his investigation.

'It is with a trembling hand I write to you,' Mrs Petley had written. 'I am an invalid with lung trouble, a young mother, with three children. I will shock you, I know, but I know I am the last person to see Joan alive and the last one to talk to her.'

Under a rigorous cross-examination, however, Mrs Petley admitted that her information was not totally correct. She had not spoken to Joan. And there was another problem with her letter. She had said that she had seen the couple on Sunday 1 August, but now in court she had changed her mind. It was 31 July when she had seen them.

Joan Woodhouse.

'Why do you now claim that this encounter took place on Saturday, 31 July, when you wrote to Mr Jacks that it happened on Sunday, 1 August?' she was asked.

Mrs Petley's answers were unconvincing. She tried to explain what had occurred. When she told the police about seeing Wade in the park, they said that the murder had happened on a Sunday. They insisted that Joan's movements on the Saturday were accounted for. A detective sergeant who was called as a witness said that Mrs Petley had come to the station with information shortly after the body was found. At that time she said that she had seen the couple on Saturday 24 July, a week before Joan disappeared. She had been very confident that that was the date. Was she not, Vincent Jackson implied, simply motivated by the reward money put up by the aunts?

As for Mrs Bidwell, the home help, Jackson made short work of her. She remembered that on several days in late July she had been in the park with Mrs Petley and her children. She had told the police that she remembered the girl in the park because of the dress she was wearing. She had admired it so much that later she bought the same type of dress. Jackson was able to point out the date on which Mrs Bidwell bought her dress – 27 July, four days before Joan Woodhouse's disappearance.

In a brilliant summing up, Jackson submitted that his client had no case to answer. There was no evidence which could possibly lead to his conviction. Had the prosecution any firm evidence about the exact date on which Joan Woodhouse died? Could they put their hands on their hearts and swear it was 31 July? Or was there some doubt?

And who could say why Joan went to Arundel and not Barnsley? Before leaving the hostel had she arranged a secret week-end assignation with someone? Or had she fully intended going to Barnsley when she left the hostel but met someone on the way whom she had gone off with? Were these not plausible possibilities, Jackson asked.

In Mrs Petley's case, Jackson dismissed her contribution to the prosecution as worthless. What reliance, he asked, could be placed on such inaccurate witness statements as hers?

Keith Simpson's report was treated with greater respect but the queries that Spooner had aired about the lack of bruising on the arms also concerned Jackson. And if Joan had been startled and had run away from her attacker, surely she would have screamed and surely someone would have heard her.

One of the most significant items of evidence was pubic hair found on Joan's brassiere. Forensic tests had proved that they were not hers. They must be from her murderer, Jackson suggested, but the same forensic tests proved that they were not Alan Wade's. And therefore . . .

After a four-day hearing the five magistrates were of the unanimous opinion that there was insufficient evidence to commit Wade for trial. Admittedly the DPP had not been enthusiastic about being involved in the hearing, for they had agreed with Spooner's conclusion about the weakness of the evidence.

Wade ended up with 40 guineas costs and he sold his story to a newspaper for £200. His solicitor's costs were £249, so there was a net loss of £9, which seems not an excessive charge given the circumstances.

The Woodhouse family were still not satisfied. They complained that the prosecution had been half-hearted and applied to Mr Justice Humphreys at

Alan Wade, his head covered by a raincoat, on his way to Arundel Magistrates' Court.

Lewes Assize Court for a Bill of Indictment. Mr Bass, who had appeared for the prosecution, had, right at the opening of the case, admitted that the evidence was purely circumstantial and this had done little more than invite a dismissal of the charge. But the Attorney-General now insisted that the case had gone as far as it could. The police had not found any evidence strong enough to lay charges against anyone.

There was one last attempt to clear up the mystery of Joan Woodhouse's death. A third police officer reviewed the evidence in 1956. He arrived at the same conclusion as Detective Superintendent Spooner – suicide.

But it is a case to which many still return. It is at the same time both intriguing and unsatisfactory. Was it really suicide? Was Alan Wade the murderer? Or another man? And why did Joan Woodhouse make her fateful decision to go to Arundel?

Note: In this account of the Joan Woodhouse case the name of the man who was suspected of murdering her has been changed.

BIBLIOGRAPHY

ABBREVIATIONS

PRO   Public Record Office
ESRO   East Sussex Record Office
WSRO West Sussex Record Office

NEWSPAPERS & MAGAZINES

Brighton & Hove Herald
Daily Express
Daily Mail
Daily Telegraph
Eastbourne Gazette
Hampshire Telegraph
News of the World
Sunday Dispatch
Sussex Advertiser
Sussex Agricultural Express
Sussex County Magazine
Sussex Daily News
Sussex Times
The Times

BOOKS & ARTICLES

1.   *The Murders of Chater & Galley*

WSRO Add Mss 24,113
WSRO Goodwood Ms 155
A Gentleman of Chichester, *Smuggling and Smugglers in Sussex: The Genuine History of the Inhuman and Unparallel'd Murders Committed on the Bodies of Mr William Galley, A Custom-House Officer in the Port of Southampton: And Mr Daniel Chater, A Shoemaker of Fordingbridge in Hampshire Written by a Gentleman of Chichester*, B. Dickinson, 1749

J.L. Rayner and G.T. Crook (eds), *The Complete Newgate Calendar*, The Navarre
    Society, 1926
F.F. Nicholls, *Honest Thieves*, Heinemann, 1973
Lord Teignmouth and C.G. Harper, *The Smugglers*, publisher not known, 1923
Geoffrey Hufton, *Scarecrow's Legion*, Rochester Press, 1983
Proceedings of the Old Bailey 1674 to 1834, www.oldbaileyonline, 2003

2.   *Sally Churchman's 'Snuff'*

J.L. Rayner and G.T. Crook (eds), *The Complete Newgate Calendar*, The Navarre
    Society, 1926
William Albery, *A Millennium of Facts in the History of Horsham and Sussex*,
    privately pubd, 1947

3.   *The Body in Gladish Wood*

ESRO Burwash Vestry Minute Book 1826–1827
ESRO Par. 284/12/1
ESRO R/L/24/1
E. Cecil Curwen (ed.), *Journal of Gideon Mantell*, OUP, 1940
Roger Wells (ed.), *Victorian Village: the Diaries of the Revd John Coker Egerton*,
    Alan Sutton, 1992

4.   *The Dismemberment in Donkey Row*

John Holloway, *An Authentic and Faithful History of the Atrocious Murder of Celia
    Holloway . . . published by his own Desire for the Benefit of Young People*, 1832
Sue Farrant, *Georgian Brighton – 1740–1820*, University of Sussex, 1980
W.H. Johnson, *Brighton's First Trunk Murderer*, Downsway Books, 1995
Clifford Musgrave, *Life in Brighton*, Hallewell, 1981
Lord Teignmouth and C.G. Harper, *The Smugglers*, publisher not known, 1923
Geoffrey Hufton, *Scarecrow's Legion*, Rochester Press, 1983

5.   *Fagan's Last Case*

ESRO QAC/3/E1/1-6
R.V. Kyrke, *History of East Sussex Constabulary 1840–1967*, self-pubd, 1967
Ringmer History Society Magazine, article by John Kay, 1986

6.   *All for a Roll of Carpet*

ESRO SPA 1/6/9
William Albery, *A Millennium of Facts in the History of Horsham and Sussex*,
    privately pubd, 1947
G.S. Jenks, *On the Sanitary Condition of Brighton – 1840*, BPP, 1842

Henry Burstow, *Reminiscences of Horsham*, FCCBS, 1911
Journal of the Police History Society, No. 16, article by David Spector, 2001

7.   *The Onion Pie Murder*

Chiddingly Vestry Minute Book 1851–1852
W.H. Johnson, *The Onion Pie Murder*, Downsway Books, 1995
J.R. Vickers, *Religious Survey of Sussex – 1851*, SRS, 1989

8.   *The Enys Road Murders*

ESRO COR/1/3/12-15

9.   *When Two Strangers Met*

PRO ASSI 36/48
John J. Eddleston, *Murderous Sussex*, Breedon Books, 1997

10.   *The Dancing Waiter*

ESRO SPA 11/3/4
Leonard Knowles, *Court of Drama*, Long, 1966
Douglas G. Browne and Tom Tullett, *Bernard Spilsbury: His Life and Cases*, Harrap, 1951
'Master Detective', article by A.W. Moss, June 2004
Real Life Crimes, No. 39, article by Paul Williams

11.   *The Arundel Park Case*

PRO MEPO 3/3022
Iain Adamson, *The Great Detective*, Frederick Muller, 1966
Keith Simpson, *Forty Years of Murder*, Harrap, 1978
Fred Narborough, *Murder on my Mind*, Wingate, 1959
Murder Most Foul, No. 47, article by Richard Terry, 2003
Journal of the Police History Society, No. 18, article by Clifford Williams, 2003

INDEX